Ben Stacy Jerrik (Ed.)

Network Forensics

Ben Stacy Jerrik (Ed.)

Network Forensics

Digital forensics, Computer network, Intrusion detection system

Part Press

Imprint

Permission is granted to copy, distribute and/or modify this document under the terms of the GNU Free Documentation License, Version 1.2 or any later version published by the Free Software Foundation; with no Invariant Sections, with the Front-Cover Texts, and with the Back- Cover Texts. A copy of the license is included in the section entitled "GNU Free Documentation License".

All parts of this book are extracted from Wikipedia, the free encyclopedia (www.wikipedia.org).

You can get detailed informations about the authors of this collection of articles at the end of this book. The editors (Ed.) of this book are no authors. They have not modified or extended the original texts.

Pictures published in this book can be under different licences than the GNU Free Documentation License. You can get detailed informations about the authors and licences of pictures at the end of this book.

The content of this book was generated collaboratively by volunteers. Please be advised that nothing found here has necessarily been reviewed by people with the expertise required to provide you with complete, accurate or reliable information. Some information in this book maybe misleading or wrong. The Publisher does not guarantee the validity of the information found here. If you need specific advice (f.e. in fields of medical, legal, financial, or risk management questions) please contact a professional who is licensed or knowledgeable in that area.

Any brand names and product names mentioned in this book are subject to trademark, brand or patent protection and are trademarks or registered trademarks of their respective holders. The use of brand names, product names, common names, trade names, product descriptions etc. even without a particular marking in this works is in no way to be construed to mean that such names may be regarded as unrestricted in respect of trademark and brand protection legislation and could thus be used by anyone.

Cover image: www.ingimage.com
Concerning the licence of the cover image please contact ingimage.

Publisher:
Part Press is a trademark of
International Book Market Service Ltd., 17 Rue Meldrum, Beau Bassin, 1713-01 Mauritius
Email: info@bookmarketservice.com
Website: www.bookmarketservice.com

Published in 2012

Printed in: U.S.A., U.K., Germany. This book was not produced in Mauritius.

ISBN: 978-613-6-11451-4

Contents

Network_forensics

Network forensics is a sub-branch of digital forensics relating to the monitoring and analysis of computer network traffic for the purposes of information gathering, legal evidence, or intrusion detection.[1] Unlike other areas of digital forensics, network investigations deal with volatile and dynamic information. Network traffic is transmitted and then lost, so network forensics is often a pro-active investigation.[2]

Network forensics generally has two uses. The first, relating to security, involves monitoring a network for anomalous traffic and identifying intrusions. An attacker might be able to erase all log files on a compromised host; network-based evidence might therefore be the only evidence available for forensic analysis.[3] The second form of Network forensics relates to law enforcement. In this case analysis of captured network traffic can include tasks such as reassembling transferred files, searching for keywords and parsing human communication such as emails or chat sessions.

Two systems are commonly used to collect network data; a brute force "catch it as you can" and a more intelligent "stop look listen" method.

Overview

Network forensics is a comparatively new field of forensic science. The growing popularity of the Internet in homes means that computing has become network-centric and data is now available outside of disk-based digital evidence. Network forensics can be performed as a standalone investigation or alongside a computer forensics analysis (where it is often used to reveal links between digital devices or reconstruct how a crime was committed).[2]

Marcus Ranum is credited with defining Network forensics as "the capture, recording, and analysis of network events in order to discover the source of security attacks or other problem incidents."[4]

Compared to computer forensics, where evidence is usually preserved on disk, network data is more volatile and unpredictable. Investigators often only have material to examine if packet filters, firewalls, and intrusion detection systems were set up to anticipate breaches of security.[2]

Systems used to collect network data for forensics use usually come in two forms:[5]

- "Catch-it-as-you-can" - This is where all packets passing through certain traffic point are captured and written to storage with analysis being done subsequently in batch mode. This approach requires large amounts of storage.
- "Stop, look and listen" - This is where each packet is analyzed in a rudimentary way in memory and only certain information saved for future analysis. This approach requires a faster processor to keep up with incoming traffic.

Types

Ethernet

Applying forensic methods on the Ethernet layer is done by eavesdropping bit streams with tools called monitoring tools or sniffers. The most common tools on this layer is Wireshark (formerly known as Ethereal). It collects all data on this layer and allow the user to filter for different events. With these tools websites, email attachments and more that has been transmitted over the network can be reconstructed. An advantage of collecting this data is that it is directly connected to a host. If, for example the IP address or the MAC address of a host at a certain time is known, all data for or from this IP or MAC address can be filtered.

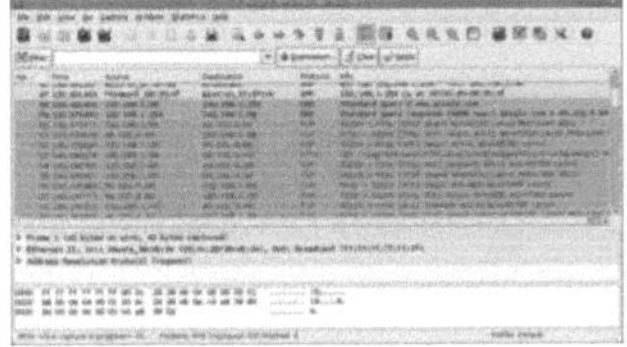

Wireshark, a common tool used to monitor and record network traffic

To establish the connection between IP and MAC address, it is useful to take a closer look at auxiliary network protocols. The Address Resolution Protocol (ARP) tables list the MAC addresses with the corresponding IP addresses.

To collect data on this layer, the network interface card (NIC) of a host can be put into "promiscuous mode". By this, it collects all traffic that comes over the network not only the traffic meant for this special host.

However, if an intruder or attacker is aware that his connection might be eavesdropped, he might use encryption to secure his connection. It is almost impossible to break nowadays encryption but the fact that a suspect's connection to another host is all the time encrypted might indicate that the other host is an accomplice of the suspect.

TCP/IP

On the network layer the Internet Protocol (IP) is responsible for directing the packets generated by TCP through the network (e.g., the Internet) by adding source and destination information which can be interpreted by routers all over the network. Cellular digital packet networks, like GPRS, use similar protocols like IP, so the methods described for IP work with them as well.

For the correct routing, every intermediate router must have a routing table to know where to send the packet next. These routing tables are one of the best sources of information if investigating a digital crime and trying to track down an attacker. To do this, it is necessary to follow the packets of the attacker, reverse the sending route and find the computer the packet came from (i.e., the attacker).

Another source of evidence on this layer are authentication logs. They show which account and which user was associated with an activity and may reveal who was the attacker or at least sets limits to the people who come into consideration of being the attacker.

The Internet

The internet can be a rich source of digital evidence including web browsing, email, newsgroup, synchronous chat and peer-to-peer traffic. For example web server logs can be used to show when (or if) a suspect accessed information related to criminal activity. Email accounts can often contain useful evidence; but email headers are easily faked and, so, network forensics may be used to prove the exact origin of incriminating material. Network forensics can also be used in order to find out who is using a particular computer[6] by extracting user account information from the network traffic.

Wireless forensics

Wireless forensics is a sub-discipline of network forensics. The main goal of wireless forensics is to provide the methodology and tools required to collect and analyze (wireless) network traffic that can be presented as valid digital evidence in a court of law. The evidence collected can correspond to plain data or, with the broad usage of Voice-over-IP (VoIP) technologies, especially over wireless, can include voice conversations.

Analysis of wireless network traffic is similar to that on wired networks, however there may be the added consideration of wireless security measures.

References

[1] Gary Palmer, A Road Map for Digital Forensic Research, Report from DFRWS 2001, First Digital Forensic Research Workshop, Utica, New York, August 7 − 8, 2001, Page(s) 27−30

[2] Casey, Eoghan (2004). *Digital Evidence and Computer Crime, Second Edition* (http://books.google.co.uk/books?id=Xo8GMt_AbQsC& hl=en&dq=Digital Evidence and Computer Crime, Second Edition&ei=it1XTMncCMm44gbC_qyFBw&sa=X&oi=book_result& ct=result&resnum=1&ved=0CDQQ6AEwAA). Elsevier. ISBN 0-12-163104-4. .

[3] Erik Hjelmvik, Passive Network Security Analysis with NetworkMiner http://www.forensicfocus.com/ passive-network-security-analysis-networkminer

[4] Marcus Ranum, Network Flight Recorder, http://www.ranum.com

[5] Simson Garfinkel, Network Forensics: Tapping the Internet http://www.oreillynet.com/pub/a/network/2002/04/26/nettap.html

[6] "Facebook, SSL and Network Forensics", NETRESEC Network Security Blog, 2011 (http://www.netresec.com/?page=Blog& month=2011-01&post=Facebook-SSL-and-Network-Forensics)

External links

- Forensics Wiki (http://www.forensicswiki.org/wiki/Tools:Network_Forensics)
- Network Forensic Tools, Network Computing December 3, 2004 (http://www.networkcomputing.com/ data-protection/network-forensic-tools.php?p=11)

adit

Digital_forensics

Digital forensics (sometimes known as **digital forensic science**) is a branch of forensic science encompassing the recovery and investigation of material found in digital devices, often in relation to computer crime.[1] [2] The term digital forensics was originally used as a synonym for computer forensics but has expanded to cover investigation of all devices capable of storing digital data.[1] With roots in the personal computing revolution of the late 1970s and early '80s, the discipline evolved in a haphazard manner during the 1990s, and it was not until the early 21st century that national policies emerged.

Aerial photo of FLETC, where US digital forensics standards were developed in the 1980s and '90s

Digital forensics investigations have a variety of applications. The most common is to support or refute a hypothesis before criminal or civil (as part of the electronic discovery process) courts. Forensics may also feature in the private sector; such as during internal corporate investigations or intrusion investigation (a specialist probe into the nature and extent of an unauthorized network intrusion).

The technical aspect of an investigation is divided into several sub-branches, relating to the type of digital devices involved; computer forensics, network forensics, database forensics and mobile device forensics. The typical forensic process encompasses the seizure, forensic imaging (acquisition) and analysis of digital media and the production of a report into collected evidence.

As well as identifying direct evidence of a crime, digital forensics can be used to attribute evidence to specific suspects, confirm alibis or statements, determine intent, identify sources (for example, in copyright cases), or authenticate documents.[3] Investigations are much broader in scope than other areas of forensic analysis (where the usual aim is to provide answers to a series of simpler questions) often involving complex time-lines or hypotheses.[4]

History

Prior to the 1980s crimes involving computers were dealt with using existing laws. The first computer crimes were recognized in the 1978 Florida Computer Crimes Act, which included legislation against the unauthorized modification or deletion of data on a computer system.[5] [6] Over the next few years the range of computer crimes being committed increased, and laws were passed to deal with issues of copyright, privacy/harassment (e.g., cyber bullying, cyber stalking, and online predators) and child pornography.[7] [8] It was not until the 1980s that federal laws began to incorporate computer offences. Canada was the first country to pass legislation in 1983.[6] This was followed by the US Federal *Computer Fraud and Abuse Act* in 1986, Australian amendments to their crimes acts in 1989 and the British *Computer Abuse Act* in 1990.[6] [8]

1980s–1990s: Growth of the field

The growth in computer crime during the 1980s and 1990s caused law enforcement agencies to begin establishing specialized groups, usually at the national level, to handle the technical aspects of investigations. For example, in 1984 the FBI launched a *Computer Analysis and Response Team* and the following year a computer crime department was set up within the British Metropolitan Police fraud squad. As well as being law enforcement professionals, many of the early members of these groups were also computer hobbyists and became responsible for the field's initial research and direction.[9] [10]

One of the first practical (or at least publicised) examples of digital forensics was Cliff Stoll's pursuit of hacker Markus Hess in 1986. Stoll, whose investigation made use of computer and network forensic techniques, was not a specialised examiner.[11] Many of the earliest forensic examinations followed the same profile.[12]

Throughout the 1990s there was high demand for the these new, and basic, investigative resources. The strain on central units lead to the creation of regional, and even local, level groups to help handle the load. For example, the British National Hi-Tech Crime Unit was set up in 2001 to provide a national infrastructure for computer crime; with personnel located both centrally in London and with the various regional police forces (the unit was folded into the Serious Organised Crime Agency (SOCA) in 2006).[10]

During this period the science of digital forensics grew from the ad-hoc tools and techniques developed by these hobbyist practitioners. This is in contrast to other forensics disciplines which developed from work by the scientific community.[1] [13] It was not until 1992 that the term "computer forensics" was used in academic literature (although prior to this it had been in informal use); a paper by Collier and Spaul attempted to justify this new discipline to the forensic science world.[14] [15] This swift development resulted in a lack of standardization and training. In his 1995 book, *"High-Technology Crime: Investigating Cases Involving Computers"*, K Rosenblatt wrote:[6]

> Seizing, preserving, and analyzing evidence stored on a computer is the greatest forensic challenge facing law enforcement in the 1990s. Although most forensic tests, such as fingerprinting and DNA testing, are performed by specially trained experts the task of collecting and analyzing computer evidence is often assigned to patrol officers and detectives.[16]

2000s: Developing standards

Since 2000, in response to the need for standardization, various bodies and agencies have published guidelines for digital forensics. The Scientific Working Group on Digital Evidence (SWGDE) produced a 2002 paper, *"Best practices for Computer Forensics"*, this was followed, in 2005, by the publication of an ISO standard (ISO 17025, *General requirements for the competence of testing and calibration laboratories*).[6] [17] [18] A European lead international treaty, the Convention on Cybercrime, came into force in 2004 with the aim of reconciling national computer crime laws, investigative techniques and international co-operation. The treaty has been signed by 43 nations (including the US, Canada, Japan, South Africa, UK and other European nations) and ratified by 16.

The issue of training also received attention. Commercial companies (often forensic software developers) began to offer certification programs and digital forensic analysis was included as a topic at the UK specialist investigator training facility, Centrex.[6] [10]

Since the late 1990s mobile devices have become more widely available, advancing beyond simple communication devices, and have been found to be rich forms of information, even for crime not traditionally associated with digital forensics.[19] Despite this, digital analysis of phones has lagged behind traditional computer media, largely due to problems over the proprietary nature of devices.[20]

Focus has also shifted onto internet crime, particularly the risk of cyber warfare and cyberterrorism. A February 2010 report by the United States Joint Forces Command concluded:

> Through cyberspace, enemies will target industry, academia, government, as well as the military in the air, land, maritime, and space domains. In much the same way that airpower transformed the battlefield of World War II, cyberspace has fractured the physical barriers that shield a nation from attacks on its commerce and communication.[21]

The field of digital forensics still faces unresolved issues. A 2009 paper, "Digital Forensic Research: The Good, the Bad and the Unaddressed", by Peterson and Shenoi identified a bias towards Windows operating systems in digital forensics research.[22] In 2010 Simson Garfinkel identified issues facing digital investigations in the future, including the increasing size of digital media, the wide availability of encryption to consumers, a growing variety of operating systems and file formats, an increasing number of individuals owning multiple devices, and legal limitations on investigators. The paper also identified continued training issues, as well as the prohibitively high cost of entering the field.[11]

Development of forensic tools

During the 1980s very few specialized digital forensic tools existed, and consequently investigators often performed live analysis on media, examining computers from within the operating system using existing sysadmin tools to extract evidence. This practice carried the risk of modifying data on the disk, either inadvertently or otherwise, which led to claims of evidence tampering. A number of tools were created during the early 1990s to address the problem.

The need for such software was first recognized in 1989 at the Federal Law Enforcement Training Center, resulting in the creation of IMDUMP (by Michael White) and in 1990, SafeBack (developed by Sydex). Similar software was developed in other countries; DIBS (a hardware and software solution) was released commercially in the UK in 1991, and Rob McKemmish released *Fixed Disk Image* free to Australian law enforcement.[9] These tools allowed examiners to create an exact copy of a piece of digital media to work on, leaving the original disk intact for verification. By the end of the '90s, as demand for digital evidence grew more advanced commercial tools such as EnCase and FTK were developed, allowing analysts to examine copies of media without using any live forensics.[6] More recently, a trend towards "live memory forensics" has grown resulting in the availability of tools such as WindowsSCOPE.

More recently the same progression of tool development has occurred for mobile devices; initially investigators accessed data directly on the device, but soon specialist tools such as XRY or Radio Tactics Aceso appeared.[6]

Forensic process

A digital forensic investigation commonly consists of 3 stages: acquisition or imaging of exhibits, analysis, and reporting.[6] [23] Acquisition involves creating an exact sector level duplicate (or "forensic duplicate") of the media, often using a write blocking device to prevent modification of the original. Both acquired image and original media are hashed (using SHA-1 or MD5) and the values compared to verify the copy is accurate.[24]

During the analysis phase an investigator recovers evidence material using a number of different methodologies and tools. In 2002, an article in the *International Journal of Digital Evidence* referred to this step as "an in-depth systematic search of evidence related to the suspected crime".[1] In 2006, forensics researcher Brian Carrie described an "intuitive procedure" in which obvious evidence is first identified and then "exhaustive searches are conducted to start filling in the holes".[4]

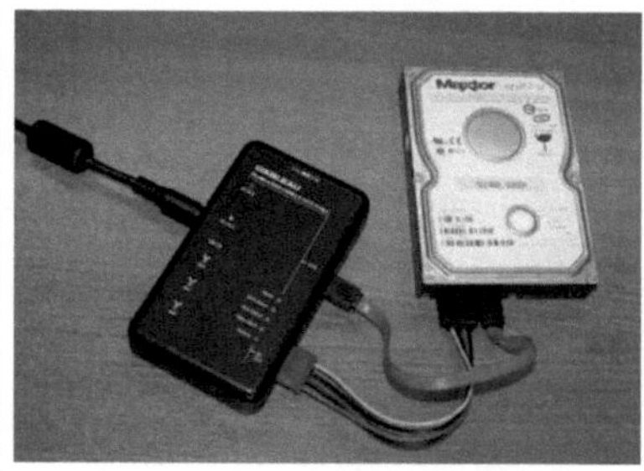
A portable Tableau write-blocker attached to a hard drive

The actual process of analysis can vary between investigations, but common methodologies include conducting keyword searches across the digital media (within files as well as unallocated and slack space), recovering deleted files and extraction of registry information (for example to list user accounts, or attached USB devices).

The evidence recovered is analysed to reconstruct events or actions and to reach conclusions, work that can often be performed by less specialised staff.[1] When an investigation is complete the data is presented, usually in the form of a written report, in lay persons' terms.[1]

Application

Digital forensics is commonly used in both criminal law and private investigation. Traditionally it has been associated with criminal law, where evidence is collected to support or oppose a hypothesis before the courts. As with other areas of forensics this is often as part of a wider investigation spanning a number of disciplines. In some cases the collected evidence is used as a form of intelligence gathering, used for other purposes than court proceedings (for example to locate, identify or halt other crimes). As a result intelligence gathering is sometimes held to a less strict forensic standard.

Camera manufacturer	Canon
Camera model	Canon EOS 400D DIGITAL
Exposure time	1/60 sec (0.016666666666667)
F-number	f/4.5
ISO speed rating	400
Date and time of data generation	11:06, August 27, 2010
Lens focal length	31 mm
Show extended details	

An example of an image's Exif metadata that might be used to prove its origin

In civil litigation or corporate matters digital forensics forms part of the electronic discovery (or eDiscovery) process. Forensic procedures are similar to those used in criminal investigations, often with different legal requirements and limitations. Outside of the courts digital forensics can form a part of internal corporate investigations.

A common example might be following unauthorized network intrusion. A specialist forensic examination into the nature and extent of the attack is performed as a damage limitation exercise. Both to establish the extent of any intrusion and in an attempt to identify the attacker.[3] [4] Such attacks were commonly conducted over phone lines during the 1980s, but in the modern era are usually propagated over the internet.[25]

The main focus of digital forensics investigations is to recover objective evidence of a criminal activity (termed actus reus in legal parlance). However, the diverse range of data held in digital devices can help with other areas of inquiry.[3]

Attribution

Meta data and other logs can be used to attribute actions to an individual. For example, personal documents on a computer drive might identify its owner.

Alibis and statements

Information provided by those involved can be cross checked with digital evidence. For example, during the investigation into the Soham murders the offender's alibi was disproved when mobile phone records of the person he claimed to be with showed she was out of town at the time.

Intent

As well as finding objective evidence of a crime being committed, investigations can also be used to prove the intent (known by the legal term mens rea). For example, the Internet history of convicted killer Neil Entwistle included references to a site discussing *How to kill people*.

Evaluation of source

File artifacts and meta-data can be used to identify the origin of a particular piece of data; for example, older versions of Microsoft Word embedded a Global Unique Identifer into files which identified the computer it had been created on. Proving whether a file was produced on the digital device being examined or obtained from elsewhere (e.g., the Internet) can be very important.[3]

Document authentication

Related to "Evaluation of Source", meta data associated with digital documents can be easily modified (for example, by changing the computer clock you can affect the creation date of a file). Document authentication relates to detecting and identifying falsification of such details.

Limitations

One major limitation to a forensic investigation is the use of encryption; this disrupts initial examination where pertinent evidence might be located using keywords. Laws to compel individuals to disclose encryption keys are still relatively new and controversial.[11]

Legal considerations

The examination of digital media is covered by national and international legislation. For civil investigations, in particular, laws may restrict the abilities of analysts to undertake examinations. Restrictions against network monitoring, or reading of personal communications often exist.[26] During criminal investigation, national laws restrict how much information can be seized.[26] For example, in the United Kingdom seizure of evidence by law enforcement is governed by the PACE act.[6] The "International Organization on Computer Evidence" (IOCE) is one agency that works to establish compatible international standards for the seizure of evidence.[27]

In the UK the same laws covering computer crime can also affect forensic investigators. The 1990 computer misuse act legislates against unauthorised access to computer material; this is a particular concern for civil investigators who have more limitations than law enforcement.

An individuals right to privacy is one area of digital forensics which is still largely undecided by courts. The US Electronic Communications Privacy Act places limitations on the ability of law enforcement or civil investigators to intercept and access evidence. The act makes a distinction between stored communication (e.g. email archives) and transmitted communication (such as VOIP). The latter, being considered more of a privacy invasion, is harder to obtain a warrant for.[6] [16] The ECPA also affects the ability of companies to investigate the computers and communications of their employees, an aspect that is still under debate as to the extent to which a company can perform such monitoring.[6]

Article 5 of the European Convention on Human Rights asserts similar privacy limitations to the ECPA and limits the processing and sharing of personal data both within the EU and with external countries. The ability of UK law enforcement to conduct digital forensics investigations is legislated by the Regulation of Investigatory Powers Act.[6]

Digital evidence

When used in a court of law digital evidence falls under the same legal guidelines as other forms of evidence; courts do not usually require more stringent guidelines.[6] [28] In the United States the Federal Rules of Evidence are used to evaluate the admissibility of digital evidence, the United Kingdom PACE and Civil Evidence acts have similar guidelines and many other countries have their own laws. US federal laws restrict seizures to items with only obvious evidential value. This is acknowledged as not always being possible to establish with digital media prior to an examination.[26]

Digital evidence can come in a number of forms

Laws dealing with digital evidence are concerned with two issues: integrity and authenticity. Integrity is ensuring that the act of seizing and acquiring digital media does not modify the evidence (either the original or the copy). Authenticity refers to the ability to confirm the integrity of information; for example that the imaged media matches the original evidence.[26] The ease with which digital media can be modified means that documenting the chain of custody from the crime scene, through analysis and, ultimately, to the court, (a form of audit trail) is important to establish the authenticity of evidence.[6]

Attorneys have argued that because digital evidence can theoretically be altered it undermines the reliability of the evidence. US judges are beginning to reject this theory, in the case *US v. Bonallo* the court ruled that "the fact that it is possible to alter data contained in a computer is plainly insufficient to establish untrustworthiness".[6] [29] In the United Kingdom guidelines such as those issued by ACPO are followed to help document the authenticity and integrity of evidence.

Digital investigators, particularly in criminal investigations, have to ensure that conclusions are based upon factual evidence and their own expert knowledge.[6] In the US, for example, Federal Rules of Evidence state that a qualified expert may testify "in the form of an opinion or otherwise" so long as:

> (1) the testimony is based upon sufficient facts or data, (2) the testimony is the product of reliable principles and methods, and (3) the witness has applied the principles and methods reliably to the facts of the case.[30]

The sub-branches of digital forensics may each have their own specific guidelines for the conduct of investigations and the handling of evidence. For example, mobile phones may be required to be placed in a Faraday shield during seizure or acquisition to prevent further radio traffic to the device. In the UK forensic examination of computers in criminal matters is subject to ACPO guidelines.[6]

Investigative tools

The admissibility of digital evidence relies on the tools used to extract it. In the US, forensic tools are subjected to the Daubert standard, where the judge is responsible for ensuring that the processes and software used were acceptable. In a 2003 paper Brian Carrier argued that the Daubert guidelines required the code of forensic tools to be published and peer reviewed. He concluded that "open source tools may more clearly and comprehensively meet the guideline requirements than would closed source tools".[31]

Branches

Digital forensics includes several sub-branches relating to the investigation of various types of devices, media or artefacts.

Computer forensics

The goal of computer forensics is to explain the current state of a digital artifact; such as a computer system, storage medium or electronic document.[32] The discipline usually covers computers, embedded systems (digital devices with rudimentary computing power and onboard memory) and static memory (such as USB pen drives).

Computer forensics can deal with a broad range of information; from logs (such as internet history) through to the actual files on the drive. In 2007 prosecutors used a spreadsheet recovered from the computer of Joseph E. Duncan III to show premeditation and secure the death penalty.[3] Sharon Lopatka's killer was identified in 2006 after email messages from him detailing torture and death fantasies were found on her computer.[6]

Mobile device forensics

Mobile device forensics is a sub-branch of digital forensics relating to recovery of digital evidence or data from a mobile device. It differs from Computer forensics in that a mobile device will have an inbuilt communication system (e.g. GSM) and, usually, proprietary storage mechanisms. Investigations usually focus on simple data such as call data and communications (SMS/Email) rather than in-depth recovery of deleted data.[6] [33] SMS data from a mobile device investigation helped to exonerate Patrick Lumumba in the murder of Meredith Kercher.[3]

Mobile devices are also useful for providing location information; either from inbuilt gps/location tracking or via cell site logs, which track the devices within their range. Such information was used to track down the kidnappers of Thomas Onofri in 2006.[3]

Mobile phones in a UK Evidence bag

Network forensics

Network forensics is concerned with the monitoring and analysis of computer network traffic, both local and WAN/internet, for the purposes of information gathering, evidence collection, or intrusion detection.[34] Traffic is usually intercepted at the packet level, and either stored for later analysis or filtered in real-time. Unlike other areas of digital forensics network data is often volatile and rarely logged, making the discipline often reactionary.

In 2000 the FBI lured computer hackers Aleksey Ivanov and Gorshkov to the United States for a fake job interview. By monitoring network traffic from the pair's computers, the FBI identified passwords allowing them to collect evidence directly from Russian-based computers.[6] [35]

Database forensics

Database forensics is a branch of digital forensics relating to the forensic study of databases and their metadata.[36] Investigations use database contents, log files and in-RAM data to build a time-line or recover relevant information.

See also

- Cyberspace
- Glossary of digital forensics terms
- BackTrack

Related journals

- *Journal of Digital Forensics, Security and Law* [37]
- *International Journal of Digital Crime and Forensics* [38]
- *Journal of Digital Investigation* [39]
- *International Journal of Digital Evidence* [40]
- *International Journal of Forensic Computer Science* [41]
- *Journal of Digital Forensic Practice* [42]
- *Small Scale Digital Device Forensic Journal* [43]

References

[1] M Reith, C Carr, G Gunsch (2002). "An examination of digital forensic models" (http://citeseerx.ist.psu.edu/viewdoc/summary?doi=10. 1.1.13.9683). International Journal of Digital Evidence. . Retrieved 2 August 2010.

[2] Carrier, B (2001). "Defining digital forensic examination and analysis tools" (http://citeseerx.ist.psu.edu/viewdoc/summary?doi=10.1.1. 14.8953). Digital Research Workshop II. . Retrieved 2 August 2010.

[3] Various (2009). Eoghan Casey. ed. *Handbook of Digital Forensics and Investigation* (http://books.google.co.uk/ books?id=xNjsDprqtUYC). Academic Press. p. 567. ISBN 0123742676. . Retrieved 27 August 2010.

[4] Carrier, Brian D (07). "Basic Digital Forensic Investigation Concepts" (http://www.digital-evidence.org/di_basics.html). .

[5] "Florida Computer Crimes Act" (http://www.clas.ufl.edu/docs/flcrimes/chapter2_1.html). . Retrieved 31 August 2010.

[6] Casey, Eoghan (2004). *Digital Evidence and Computer Crime, Second Edition* (http://books.google.co.uk/books?id=Xo8GMt_AbQsC). Elsevier. ISBN 0-12-163104-4. .

[7] Aaron Phillip; David Cowen, Chris Davis (2009). *Hacking Exposed: Computer Forensics* (http://books.google.co.uk/ books?id=yMdNrgSBUq0C). McGraw Hill Professional. p. 544. ISBN 0071626778. . Retrieved 27 August 2010.

[8] M, M. E.. "A Brief History of Computer Crime: A" (http://www.mekabay.com/overviews/history.pdf). Norwich University. . Retrieved 30 August 2010.

[9] Mohay, George M. (2003). *Computer and intrusion forensics*. Artechhouse. p. 395. ISBN 1580533698.

[10] Peter Sommer (January 2004). "The future for the policing of cybercrime". *Computer Fraud & Security* **2004** (1): 8–12. doi:10.1016/S1361-3723(04)00017-X. ISSN 1361-3723.

[11] Simson L. Garfinkel (August 2010). "Digital forensics research: The next 10 years". *Digital Investigation* **7**: S64-S73. doi:10.1016/j.diin.2010.05.009. ISSN 1742-2876.

[12] Linda Volonino, Reynaldo Anzaldua (2008). *Computer forensics for dummies*. For Dummies. pp. 384. ISBN 0470371919.

[13] GL Palmer, I Scientist, H View (2002). "Forensic analysis in the digital world" (https://utica.edu/academic/institutes/ecii/publications/ articles/9C4E938F-E3BE-8D16-45D0BAD68CDBE77.doc). International Journal of Digital Evidence. . Retrieved 2 August 2010.

[14] Wilding, E. (1997). *Computer Evidence: a Forensic Investigations Handbook*. London: Sweet & Maxwell. p. 236. ISBN 0421579900.

[15] Collier, P.A. and Spaul, B.J. (1992). "A forensic methodology for countering computer crime". *Computers and Law* (Intellect Books).

[16] K S Rosenblatt (1995). *High-Technology Crime: Investigating Cases Involving Computers* (http://www.ncjrs.gov/App/abstractdb/ AbstractDBDetails.aspx?id=175264). KSK Publications. ISBN 0-9648171-0-1. . Retrieved 4 August 2010.

[17] "Best practices for Computer Forensics" (http://www.swgde.org/documents/archived-documents/2004-11-15 SWGDE Best Practices for Computer Forensics v1.0.pdf). SWGDE. Archived from the original (http://swgde.org/documents/swgde2005/SWGDE Best Practices _Rev Sept 2004_.pdf) on 3 October 2010. . Retrieved 4 August 2010.

[18] "ISO/IEC 17025:2005" (http://www.iso.org/iso/catalogue_detail.htm?csnumber=39883). ISO. . Retrieved 20 August 2010.

[19] SG Punja (2008). "Mobile device analysis" (http://www.ssddfj.org/papers/SSDDFJ_V2_1_Punja_Mislan.pdf). *Small Scale Digital Device Forensics Journal*. .

[20] R Ahmed (2008). "Mobile forensics: an overview, tools, future trends and challenges from law enforcement perspective" (http://www. iceg.net/2008/books/2/34_312-323.pdf). *6th International Conference on E-Governance.* .

[21] "The Joint Operating Environment" (http://www.jfcom.mil/newslink/storyarchive/2010/JOE_2010_o.pdf), Report released, Feb. 18, 2010, pp. 34–36

[22] Peterson, Gilbert & Shenoi, Sujeet (2009). "Digital Forensic Research: The Good, the Bad and the Unaddressed". *Advances in Digital Forensics V* (Springer Boston) **306**: 17–36. doi:10.1007/978-3-642-04155-6_2.

[23] "'Electronic Crime Scene Investigation Guide: A Guide for First Responders" (http://www.ncjrs.gov/pdffiles1/nij/187736.pdf). National Institute of Justice. 2001. .

[24] Maarten Van Horenbeeck (24). "Technology Crime Investigation" (http://web.archive.org/web/20080517022757/http://www.daemon. be/maarten/forensics.html#dr). Archived from the original (http://www.daemon.be/maarten/forensics.html#dr) on 17 May 2008. . Retrieved 17 August 2010.

[25] Warren G. Kruse, Jay G. Heiser (2002). *Computer forensics: incident response essentials*. Addison-Wesley. p. 392. ISBN 0201707195.

[26] Sarah Mocas (February 2004). "Building theoretical underpinnings for digital forensics research". *Digital Investigation* **1** (1): 61–68. doi:10.1016/j.diin.2003.12.004. ISSN 1742-2876.

[27] Kanellis, Panagiotis (2006). *Digital crime and forensic science in cyberspace*. Idea Group Inc (IGI). p. 357. ISBN 1591408733.

[28] Daniel J. Ryan; Gal Shpantzer. "Legal Aspects of Digital Forensics" (http://euro.ecom.cmu.edu/program/law/08-732/Evidence/ RyanShpantzer.pdf). . Retrieved 31 August 2010.

[29] *US v. Bonallo*, 858 F. 2d 1427 (http://scholar.google.co.uk/scholar_case?case=17436631095971908840&q=US+v.+Bonallo&hl=en& as_sdt=2002&as_vis=1) (9th Cir. 1988).

[30] "Federal Rules of Evidence #702" (http://federalevidence.com/rules-of-evidence#Rule702). . Retrieved 23 August 2010.

[31] Brian Carrier (October 2002). "Open Source Digital Forensic Tools: The Legal Argument" (http://www.digital-evidence.org/papers/ opensrc_legal.pdf). @stake Research Report. .

[32] A Yasinsac; RF Erbacher, DG Marks, MM Pollitt (2003). "Computer forensics education" (http://ieeexplore.ieee.org/iel5/8013/27399/ 01219052.pdf?arnumber=1219052). IEEE Security & Privacy. . Retrieved 26 July 2010.

[33] "Technology Crime Investigation :: Mobile forensics" (http://web.archive.org/web/20080517022757/http://www.daemon.be/ maarten/forensics.html#mob). Archived from the original (http://www.daemon.be/maarten/forensics.html#mob) on 17 May 2008. . Retrieved 18 August 2010.

[34] Gary Palmer, A Road Map for Digital Forensic Research, Report from DFRWS 2001, First Digital Forensic Research Workshop, Utica, New York, August 7 – 8, 2001, Page(s) 27–30

[35] "2 Russians Face Hacking Charges" (http://www.themoscowtimes.com/news/article/2-russians-face-hacking-charges/253844.html). Moscow Times. 24. . Retrieved 3 September 2010.

[36] Olivier, Martin S. (March 2009). "On metadata context in Database Forensics" (http://www.sciencedirect.com/science/article/ B7CW4-4TSD9G6-1/2/a5031117d753054d92f2afba332eadf8). Science Direct. doi:10.1016/j.diin.2008.10.001.. . Retrieved 2 August 2010.

[37] http://www.jdfsl.org/

[38] http://www.igi-global.com/bookstore/titledetails.aspx?TitleId=1112&DetailsType=Description

[39] http://www.elsevier.com/wps/find/journaldescription.cws_home/702130/description#description

[40] http://www.utica.edu/academic/institutes/ecii/ijde/

[41] http://www.ijofcs.org/

[42] http://www.tandf.co.uk/journals/titles/15567281.asp

[43] http://www.ssddfj.org/

Further reading

- Carrier, Brian D. (February 2006). "Risks of live digital forensic analysis" (http://portal.acm.org/citation. cfm?id=1113034.1113069). *Communications of the ACM* **49** (2): 56–61. doi:10.1145/1113034.1113069. ISSN 0001-0782. Retrieved 31 August 2010.

- Kanellis, Panagiotis. *Digital crime and forensic science in cyberspace* (http://books.google.co.uk/ books?id=oK_oYhTPW2gC). IGI Publishing. p. 357. ISBN 1591408733.

- Jones, Andrew (2008). *Building a Digital Forensic Laboratory* (http://books.google.co.uk/ books?id=F5IU7XXKwCQC). Butterworth-Heinemann. p. 312. ISBN 1856175103.

- Marshell, Angus M. (2008). *Digital forensics: digital evidence in criminal investigation* (http://books.google. co.uk/books?id=MC0FPQAACAAJ). Wiley-Blackwell. p. 148. ISBN 0470517751.

- "Timeline of computer forensics" (http://www.pc-history.org/forensics.htm).

Computer_network

A **computer network**, often simply referred to as a network, is a collection of hardware components and computers interconnected by communication channels that allow sharing of resources and information.[1] Where at least one process in one device is able to send/receive data to/from at least one process residing in a remote device, then the two devices are said to be in a network.

Networks may be classified according to a wide variety of characteristics such as the medium used to transport the data, communications protocol used, scale, topology, and organizational scope.

Communications protocols define the rules and data formats for exchanging information in a computer network, and provide the basis for network programming. Well-known communications protocols are Ethernet, a hardware and link layer standard that is ubiquitous in local area networks, and the internet protocol suite, which defines a set of protocols for internetworking, i.e. for data communication between multiple networks, as well as host-to-host data transfer, and application-specific data transmission formats.

Computer networking is sometimes considered a sub-discipline of electrical engineering, telecommunications, computer science, information technology or computer engineering, since it relies upon the theoretical and practical application of these disciplines.

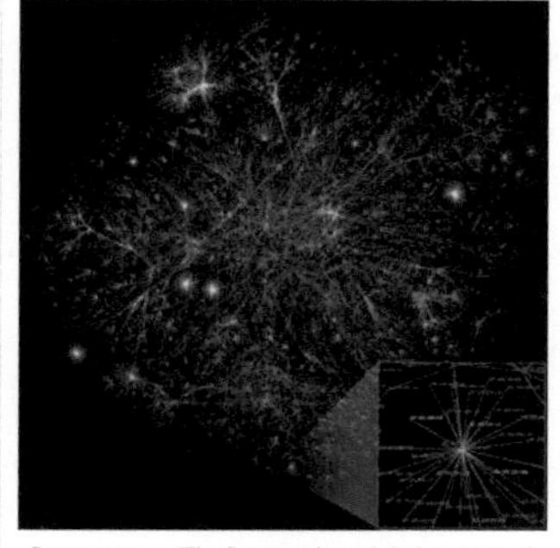

Internet map. The Internet is a global system of interconnected computer networks that use the standard Internet Protocol Suite (TCP/IP) to serve billions of users worldwide.

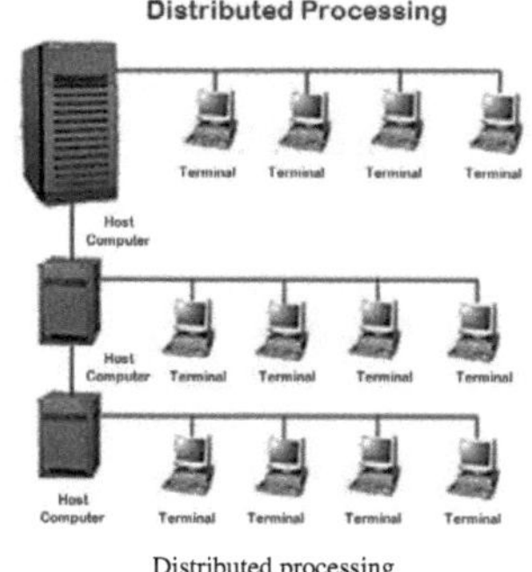

Distributed processing

History

Before the advent of computer networks that were based upon some type of telecommunications system, communication between calculation machines and early computers was performed by human users by carrying instructions between them. Many of the social behaviors seen in today's Internet were demonstrably present in the 19th century and arguably in even earlier networks using visual signals.

- In September 1940, George Stibitz used a Teletype machine to send instructions for a problem set from his Model at Dartmouth College to his Complex Number Calculator in New York and received results back by the same means. Linking output systems like teletypewriters to computers was an interest at the Advanced Research Projects Agency (ARPA) when, in 1962, J.C.R. Licklider was hired and developed a working group he called the "Intergalactic Network", a precursor to the ARPANET.

- Early networks of communicating computers included the military radar system Semi-Automatic Ground Environment (SAGE), started in the late 1950s.

- The commercial airline reservation system semi-automatic business research environment (SABRE) went online with two connected mainframes in 1960.[2] [3]

- In 1964, researchers at Dartmouth developed the Dartmouth Time Sharing System for distributed users of large computer systems. The same year, at Massachusetts Institute of Technology, a research group supported by General Electric and Bell Labs used a computer to route and manage telephone connections.

- Throughout the 1960s Leonard Kleinrock, Paul Baran and Donald Davies independently conceptualized and developed network systems which used packets that could be used in a network between computer systems.
- 1965 Thomas Merrill and Lawrence G. Roberts created the first wide area network (WAN).
- The first widely used telephone switch that used true computer control was introduced by Western Electric in 1965.
- In 1969 the University of California at Los Angeles, the Stanford Research Institute, University of California at Santa Barbara, and the University of Utah were connected as the beginning of the ARPANET network using 50 kbit/s circuits.[4]
- Commercial services using X.25 were deployed in 1972, and later used as an underlying infrastructure for expanding TCP/IP networks.

Today, computer networks are the core of modern communication. All modern aspects of the public switched telephone network (PSTN) are computer-controlled, and telephony increasingly runs over the Internet Protocol, although not necessarily the public Internet. The scope of communication has increased significantly in the past decade, and this boom in communications would not have been possible without the progressively advancing computer network. Computer networks, and the technologies needed to connect and communicate through and between them, continue to drive computer hardware, software, and peripherals industries. This expansion is mirrored by growth in the numbers and types of users of networks, from the researcher to the home user.

Properties

Computer networks:

Facilitate communications

> Using a network, people can communicate efficiently and easily via email, instant messaging, chat rooms, telephone, video telephone calls, and video conferencing.

Permit sharing of files, data, and other types of information

> In a network environment, authorized users may access data and information stored on other computers on the network. The capability of providing access to data and information on shared storage devices is an important feature of many networks.

Share network and computing resources

> In a networked environment, each computer on a network may access and use resources provided by devices on the network, such as printing a document on a shared network printer. Distributed computing uses computing resources across a network to accomplish tasks.

May be insecure

> A computer network may be used by computer hackers to deploy computer viruses or computer worms on devices connected to the network, or to prevent these devices from normally accessing the network (denial of service).

May interfere with other technologies

> Power line communication strongly disturbs certain forms of radio communication, e.g., amateur radio.[5] It may also interfere with last mile access technologies such as ADSL and VDSL.[6]

May be difficult to set up

> A complex computer network may be difficult to set up. It may also be very costly to set up an effective computer network in a large organization or company.

Communication media

Computer networks can be classified according to the hardware and associated software technology that is used to interconnect the individual devices in the network, such as electrical cable (HomePNA, power line communication, G.hn), optical fiber, and radio waves (wireless LAN). In the OSI model, these are located at levels 1 and 2.

A well-known *family* of communication media is collectively known as Ethernet. It is defined by IEEE 802 and utilizes various standards and media that enable communication between devices. Wireless LAN technology is designed to connect devices without wiring. These devices use radio waves or infrared signals as a transmission medium.

Wired technologies

The order of the following wired technologies is, roughly, from slowest to fastest transmission speed.

- *Twisted pair wire* is the most widely used medium for telecommunication. Twisted-pair cabling consist of copper wires that are twisted into pairs. Ordinary telephone wires consist of two insulated copper wires twisted into pairs. Computer networking cabling (wired Ethernet as defined by IEEE 802.3) consists of 4 pairs of copper cabling that can be utilized for both voice and data transmission. The use of two wires twisted together helps to reduce crosstalk and electromagnetic induction. The transmission speed ranges from 2 million bits per second to 10 billion bits per second. Twisted pair cabling comes in two forms: unshielded twisted pair (UTP) and shielded twisted-pair (STP). Each form comes in several category ratings, designed for use in various scenarios.

- *Coaxial cable* is widely used for cable television systems, office buildings, and other work-sites for local area networks. The cables consist of copper or aluminum wire surrounded by an insulating layer (typically a flexible material with a high dielectric constant), which itself is surrounded by a conductive layer. The insulation helps minimize interference and distortion. Transmission speed ranges from 200 million bits per second to more than 500 million bits per second.

- ITU-T G.hn technology uses existing home wiring (coaxial cable, phone lines and power lines) to create a high-speed (up to 1 Gigabit/s) local area network.

- An optical fiber is a glass fiber. It uses pulses of light to transmit data. Some advantages of optical fibers over metal wires are less transmission loss, immunity from electromagnetic radiation, and very fast tramission speed, up to trillions of bits per second. One can use different colors of lights to increase the number of messages being sent over a fiber optic cable.

Wireless technologies

- *Terrestrial microwave* – Terrestrial microwave communication uses Earth-based transmitters and receivers resembling satellite dishes. Terrestrial microwaves are in the low-gigahertz range, which limits all communications to line-of-sight. Relay stations are spaced approximately 48 km (**unknown operator: u'strong'** mi) apart.

- *Communications satellites* – The satellites communicate via microwave radio waves, which are not deflected by the Earth's atmosphere. The satellites are stationed in space, typically in geosynchronous orbit **unknown operator: u','unknown operator: u','unknown operator: u','** (**unknown operator: u'strong'unknown operator: u','**mi) above the equator. These Earth-orbiting systems are capable of receiving and relaying voice, data, and TV signals.

- *Cellular and PCS systems* use several radio communications technologies. The systems divide the region covered into multiple geographic areas. Each area has a low-power transmitter or radio relay antenna device to relay calls from one area to the next area.

- *Radio and spread spectrum technologies* – Wireless local area network use a high-frequency radio technology similar to digital cellular and a low-frequency radio technology. Wireless LANs use spread spectrum technology to enable communication between multiple devices in a limited area. IEEE 802.11 defines a common flavor of open-standards wireless radio-wave technology.

- Infrared communication can transmit signals for small distances, typically no more than 10 meters. In most cases, line-of-sight propagation is used, which limits the physical positioning of communicating devices.
- A global area network (GAN) is a network used for supporting mobile across an arbitrary number of wireless LANs, satellite coverage areas, etc. The key challenge in mobile communications is handing off user communications from one local coverage area to the next. In IEEE Project 802, this involves a succession of terrestrial wireless LANs.[7]

Exotic technologies

There have been various attempts at transporting data over more or less exotic media:

- IP over Avian Carriers was a humorous April fool's Request for Comments, issued as **RFC 1149**. It was implemented in real life in 2001.[8]
- Extending the Internet to interplanetary dimensions via radio waves.[9]

Both cases have a large round-trip delay time, which prevents useful communication.

Communications protocols and network programming

A communications protocol is a set of rules for exchanging information over a network. It is typically a protocol stack (also see the OSI model), which is a "stack" of protocols, in which each protocol uses the protocol below it. An important example of a protocol stack is HTTP running over TCP over IP over IEEE 802.11 (TCP and IP are members of the Internet Protocol Suite, and IEEE 802.11 is a member of the Ethernet protocol suite). This stack is used between the wireless router and the home user's personal computer when the user is surfing the web.

Communication protocols have various properties, such as whether they are connection-oriented or connectionless, whether they use circuit mode or packet switching, or whether they use hierarchical or flat addressing.

There are many communication protocols, a few of which are described below.

Ethernet

Ethernet is a family of connectionless protocols used in LANs, described by a set of standards together called IEEE 802 published by the Institute of Electrical and Electronics Engineers. It has a flat addressing scheme and is mostly situated at levels 1 and 2 of the OSI model. For home users today, the most well-known member of this protocol family is IEEE 802.11, otherwise known as Wireless LAN (WLAN). However, the complete protocol suite deals with a multitude of networking aspects not only for home use, but especially when the technology is deployed to support a diverse range of business needs. MAC bridging (IEEE 802.1D) deals with the routing of Ethernet packets using a Spanning Tree Protocol, IEEE 802.1Q describes VLANs, and IEEE 802.1X defines a port-based Network Access Control protocol, which forms the basis for the authentication mechanisms used in VLANs, but it is also found in WLANs – it is what the home user sees when the user has to enter a "wireless access key".

Internet Protocol Suite

The Internet Protocol Suite, often also called TCP/IP, is the foundation of all modern internetworking. It offers connection-less as well as connection-oriented services over an inherently unreliable network traversed by datagram transmission at the Internet protocol (IP) level. At its core, the protocol suite defines the addressing, identification, and routing specification in form of the traditional Internet Protocol Version 4 (IPv4) and IPv6, the next generation of the protocol with a much enlarged addressing capability.

SONET/SDH

Synchronous Optical Networking (SONET) and Synchronous Digital Hierarchy (SDH) are standardized multiplexing protocols that transfer multiple digital bit streams over optical fiber using lasers. They were originally designed to transport circuit mode communications from a variety of different sources, primarily to support real-time, uncompressed, circuit-switched voice encoded in PCM format. However, due to its protocol neutrality and transport-oriented features, SONET/SDH also was the obvious choice for transporting Asynchronous Transfer Mode (ATM) frames.

Asynchronous Transfer Mode

Asynchronous Transfer Mode (ATM) is a switching technique for telecommunication networks. It uses asynchronous time-division multiplexing and encodes data into small, fixed-sized cells. This differs from other protocols such as the Internet Protocol Suite or Ethernet that use variable sized packets or frames. ATM has similarity with both circuit and packet switched networking. This makes it a good choice for a network that must handle both traditional high-throughput data traffic, and real-time, low-latency content such as voice and video. ATM uses a connection-oriented model in which a virtual circuit must be established between two endpoints before the actual data exchange begins.

While the role of ATM is diminishing in favor of next-generation networks, it still plays a role in the last mile, which is the connection between an Internet service provider and the home user. For an interesting write-up of the technologies involved, including the deep stacking of communications protocols used, see.[10]

Network programming

Computer network programming involves writing computer programs that communicate with each other across a computer network. Different programs must be written for the client process, which initiates the communication, and for the server process, which waits for the communication to be initiated. Both endpoints of the communication flow are implemented as network sockets; hence network programming is basically socket programming.

Scale

Computer network types by geographical scope
• Near field (NFC)
• Body (BAN)
• Personal (PAN)
• Near-me (NAN)
• Local (LAN)
• Home (HAN)
• Storage (SAN)
• Campus (CAN)
• Backbone
• Metropolitan (MAN)
• Wide (WAN)
• Internet
• Interplanetary Internet

Networks are often classified by their physical or organizational extent or their purpose. Usage, trust level, and access rights differ between these types of networks.

Personal area network

A personal area network (PAN) is a computer network used for communication among computer and different information technological devices close to one person. Some examples of devices that are used in a PAN are personal computers, printers, fax machines, telephones, PDAs, scanners, and even video game consoles. A PAN may include wired and wireless devices. The reach of a PAN typically extends to 10 meters.[11] A wired PAN is usually constructed with USB and Firewire connections while technologies such as Bluetooth and infrared communication typically form a wireless PAN.

Local area network

A local area network (LAN) is a network that connects computers and devices in a limited geographical area such as home, school, computer laboratory, office building, or closely positioned group of buildings. Each computer or device on the network is a node. Current wired LANs are most likely to be based on Ethernet technology, although new standards like ITU-T G.hn also provide a way to create a wired LAN using existing home wires (coaxial cables, phone lines and power lines).[12]

All interconnected devices must understand the network layer (layer 3), because they are handling multiple subnets (the different colors). Those inside the library, which have only 10/100 Mbit/s Ethernet connections to the user device and a Gigabit Ethernet connection to the central router, could be called "layer 3 switches" because they only have Ethernet interfaces and must understand IP. It would be more correct to call them access routers, where the router at the top is a distribution router that connects to the Internet and academic networks' customer access routers.

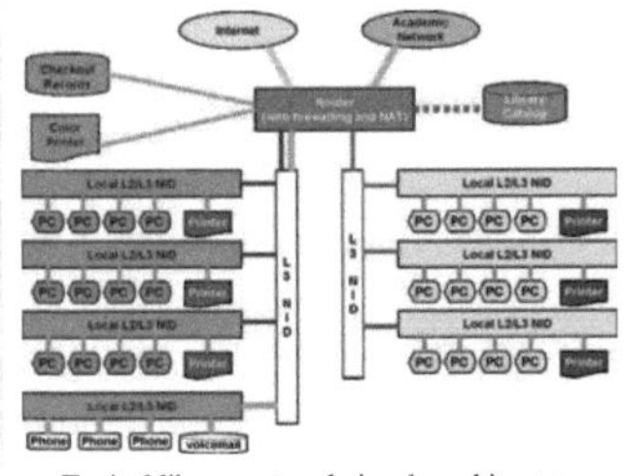

Typical library network, in a branching tree topology and controlled access to resources

The defining characteristics of LANs, in contrast to WANs (Wide Area Networks), include their higher data transfer rates, smaller geographic range, and no need for leased telecommunication lines. Current Ethernet or other IEEE 802.3 LAN technologies operate at speeds up to 10 Gbit/s. This is the data transfer rate. IEEE has projects investigating the standardization of 40 and 100 Gbit/s.[13] LANs can be connected to Wide area network by using routers.

Home area network

A home area network (HAN) is a residential LAN which is used for communication between digital devices typically deployed in the home, usually a small number of personal computers and accessories, such as printers and mobile computing devices. An important function is the sharing of Internet access, often a broadband service through a cable TV or Digital Subscriber Line (DSL) provider.

Storage area network

A storage area network (SAN) is a dedicated network that provides access to consolidated, block level data storage. SANs are primarily used to make storage devices, such as disk arrays, tape libraries, and optical jukeboxes, accessible to servers so that the devices appear like locally attached devices to the operating system. A SAN typically has its own network of storage devices that are generally not accessible through the local area network by other devices. The cost and complexity of SANs dropped in the early 2000s to levels allowing wider adoption across both enterprise and small to medium sized business environments.

Campus area network

A campus area network (CAN) is a computer network made up of an interconnection of LANs within a limited geographical area. The networking equipment (switches, routers) and transmission media (optical fiber, copper plant, Cat5 cabling etc.) are almost entirely owned (by the campus tenant / owner: an enterprise, university, government etc.).

In the case of a university campus-based campus network, the network is likely to link a variety of campus buildings including, for example, academic colleges or departments, the university library, and student residence halls.

Backbone network

A backbone network is part of a computer network infrastructure that interconnects various pieces of network, providing a path for the exchange of information between different LANs or subnetworks. A backbone can tie together diverse networks in the same building, in different buildings in a campus environment, or over wide areas. Normally, the backbone's capacity is greater than that of the networks connected to it.

A large corporation which has many locations may have a backbone network that ties all of these locations together, for example, if a server cluster needs to be accessed by different departments of a company which are located at different geographical locations. The equipment which ties these departments together constitute the network backbone. Network performance management including network congestion are critical parameters taken into account when designing a network backbone.

A specific case of a backbone network is the Internet backbone, which is the set of wide-area network connections and core routers that interconnect all networks connected to the Internet.

Metropolitan area network

A Metropolitan area network (MAN) is a large computer network that usually spans a city or a large campus.

Wide area network

A wide area network (WAN) is a computer network that covers a large geographic area such as a city, country, or spans even intercontinental distances, using a communications channel that combines many types of media such as telephone lines, cables, and air waves. A WAN often uses transmission facilities provided by common carriers, such as telephone companies. WAN technologies generally function at the lower three layers of the OSI reference model: the physical layer, the data link layer, and the network layer.

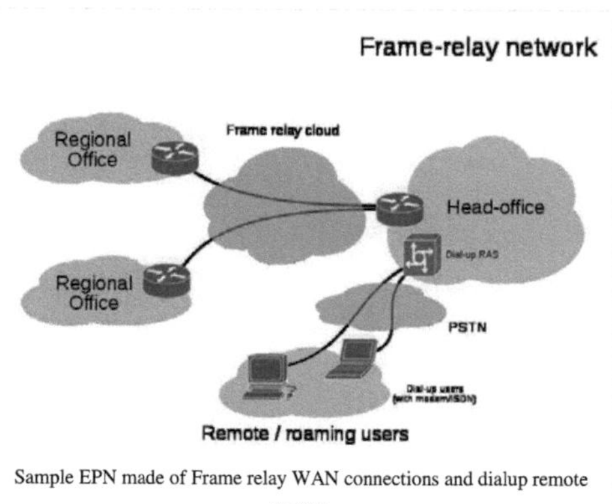

Sample EPN made of Frame relay WAN connections and dialup remote access.

Enterprise private network

An enterprise private network is a network built by an enterprise to interconnect various company sites, e.g., production sites, head offices, remote offices, shops, in order to share computer resources.

Virtual private network

A virtual private network (VPN) is a computer network in which some of the links between nodes are carried by open connections or virtual circuits in some larger network (e.g., the Internet) instead of by physical wires. The data link layer protocols of the virtual network are said to be tunneled through the larger network when this is the case. One common application is secure communications through the public Internet, but a VPN need not have explicit security features, such as authentication or content encryption. VPNs, for example, can be used to separate the traffic of different user communities over an underlying network with strong security features.

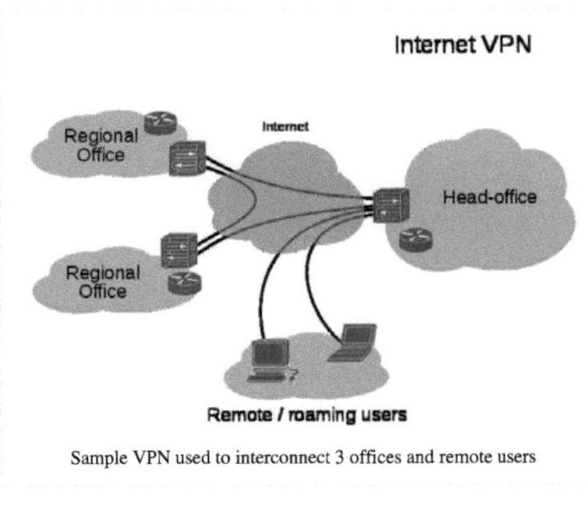

Sample VPN used to interconnect 3 offices and remote users

VPN may have best-effort performance, or may have a defined service level agreement (SLA) between the VPN customer and the VPN service provider. Generally, a VPN has a topology more complex than point-to-point.

Internetwork

An internetwork is the connection of multiple computer networks via a common routing technology using routers. The Internet is an aggregation of many connected internetworks spanning the Earth.

Organizational scope

Networks are typically managed by organizations which own them. According to the owner's point of view, networks are seen as intranets or extranets. A special case of network is the Internet, which has no single owner but a distinct status when seen by an organizational entity – that of permitting virtually unlimited global connectivity for a great multitude of purposes.

Intranets and extranets

Intranets and extranets are parts or extensions of a computer network, usually a LAN.

An intranet is a set of networks, using the Internet Protocol and IP-based tools such as web browsers and file transfer applications, that is under the control of a single administrative entity. That administrative entity closes the intranet to all but specific, authorized users. Most commonly, an intranet is the internal network of an organization. A large intranet will typically have at least one web server to provide users with organizational information.

An extranet is a network that is limited in scope to a single organization or entity and also has limited connections to the networks of one or more other usually, but not necessarily, trusted organizations or entities—a company's customers may be given access to some part of its intranet—while at the same time the customers may not be considered *trusted* from a security standpoint. Technically, an extranet may also be categorized as a CAN, MAN, WAN, or other type of network, although an extranet cannot consist of a single LAN; it must have at least one connection with an external network.

Internet

The Internet is a global system of interconnected governmental, academic, corporate, public, and private computer networks. It is based on the networking technologies of the Internet Protocol Suite. It is the successor of the Advanced Research Projects Agency Network (ARPANET) developed by DARPA of the United States Department of Defense. The Internet is also the communications backbone underlying the World Wide Web (WWW).

Participants in the Internet use a diverse array of methods of several hundred documented, and often standardized, protocols compatible with the Internet Protocol Suite and an addressing system (IP addresses) administered by the Internet Assigned Numbers Authority and address registries. Service providers and large enterprises exchange information about the reachability of their address spaces through the Border Gateway Protocol (BGP), forming a redundant worldwide mesh of transmission paths.

Network topology

Common layouts

A network topology is the layout of the interconnections of the nodes of a computer network. Common layouts are:

- A bus network: all nodes are connected to a common medium along this medium. This was the layout used in the original Ethernet, called 10BASE5 and 10BASE2.
- A star network: all nodes are connected to a special central node. This is the typical layout found in a Wireless LAN, where each wireless client connects to the central Wireless access point.
- A ring network: each node is connected to its left and right neighbour node, such that all nodes are connected and that each node can reach each other node by traversing nodes left- or rightwards. The Fiber Distributed Data Interface (FDDI) made use of such a topology.
- A mesh network: each node is connected to an arbitrary number of neighbours in such a way that there is at least one traversal from any node to any other.
- A fully connected network: each node is connected to every other node in the network.

Note that the physical layout of the nodes in a network may not necessarily reflect the network topology. As an example, with FDDI, the network topology is a ring (actually two counter-rotating rings), but the physical topology is a star, because all neighboring connections are routed via a central physical location.

Overlay network

An overlay network is a virtual computer network that is built on top of another network. Nodes in the overlay are connected by virtual or logical links, each of which corresponds to a path, perhaps through many physical links, in the underlying network. The topology of the overlay network may (and often does) differ from that of the underlying one.

For example, many peer-to-peer networks are overlay networks because they are organized as nodes of a virtual system of links run on top of the Internet. The Internet was initially built as an overlay on the telephone network.[14]

The most striking example of an overlay network, however, is the Internet itself: At the IP layer, each node can reach any other by a direct connection to the desired IP address, thereby creating a fully connected network; the underlying network, however, is composed of a mesh-like interconnect of subnetworks of varying topologies (and, in fact, technologies). Address resolution and routing are the means which allows the mapping of the fully connected IP overlay network to the underlying ones.

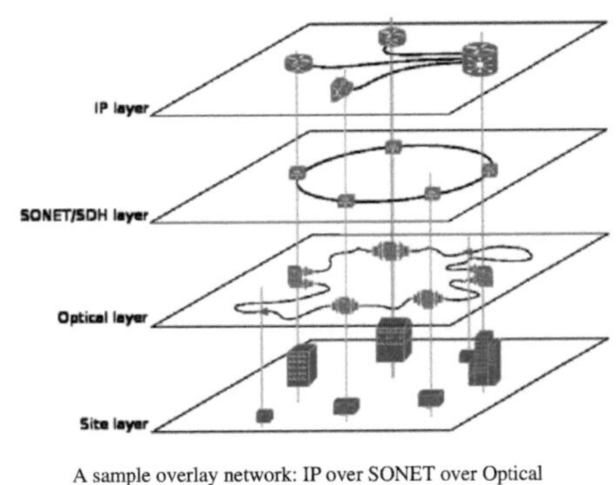

A sample overlay network: IP over SONET over Optical

Overlay networks have been around since the invention of networking when computer systems were connected over telephone lines using modems, before any data network existed.

Another example of an overlay network is a distributed hash table, which maps keys to nodes in the network. In this case, the underlying network is an IP network, and the overlay network is a table (actually a map) indexed by keys.

Overlay networks have also been proposed as a way to improve Internet routing, such as through quality of service guarantees to achieve higher-quality streaming media. Previous proposals such as IntServ, DiffServ, and IP Multicast have not seen wide acceptance largely because they require modification of all routers in the network. On the other hand, an overlay network can be incrementally deployed on end-hosts running the overlay protocol software, without cooperation from Internet service providers. The overlay has no control over how packets are routed in the underlying network between two overlay nodes, but it can control, for example, the sequence of overlay nodes a message traverses before reaching its destination.

For example, Akamai Technologies manages an overlay network that provides reliable, efficient content delivery (a kind of multicast). Academic research includes end system multicast [15] and overcast for multicast; RON (resilient overlay network) for resilient routing; and OverQoS for quality of service guarantees, among others.

Basic hardware components

Apart from the physical communications media themselves as described above, networks comprise additional basic hardware building blocks interconnecting their terminals, such as network interface cards (NICs), hubs, bridges, switches, and routers.

Network interface cards

A network card, network adapter, or NIC (network interface card) is a piece of computer hardware designed to allow computers to physically access a networking medium. It provides a low-level addressing system through the use of MAC addresses.

Each Ethernet network interface has a unique MAC address which is usually stored in a small memory device on the card, allowing any device to connect to the network without creating an address conflict. Ethernet MAC addresses are composed of six octets. Uniqueness is maintained by the IEEE, which manages the Ethernet address space by assigning 3-octet prefixes to equipment manufacturers. The list of prefixes [16] is publicly available. Each manufacturer is then obliged to both use only their assigned prefix(es) and to uniquely set the 3-octet suffix of every Ethernet interface they produce.

Repeaters and hubs

A repeater is an electronic device that receives a signal, cleans it of unnecessary noise, regenerates it, and retransmits it at a higher power level, or to the other side of an obstruction, so that the signal can cover longer distances without degradation. In most twisted pair Ethernet configurations, repeaters are required for cable that runs longer than 100 meters. A repeater with multiple ports is known as a hub. Repeaters work on the Physical Layer of the OSI model. Repeaters require a small amount of time to regenerate the signal. This can cause a propagation delay which can affect network communication when there are several repeaters in a row. Many network architectures limit the number of repeaters that can be used in a row (e.g. Ethernet's 5-4-3 rule).

Today, repeaters and hubs have been made mostly obsolete by switches (see below).

Bridges

A network bridge connects multiple network segments at the data link layer (layer 2) of the OSI model. Bridges broadcast to all ports except the port on which the broadcast was received. However, bridges do not promiscuously copy traffic to all ports, as hubs do, but learn which MAC addresses are reachable through specific ports. Once the bridge associates a port and an address, it will send traffic for that address to that port only.

Bridges learn the association of ports and addresses by examining the source address of frames that it sees on various ports. Once a frame arrives through a port, its source address is stored and the bridge assumes that MAC address is associated with that port. The first time that a previously unknown destination address is seen, the bridge will forward the frame to all ports other than the one on which the frame arrived.

Bridges come in three basic types:

- Local bridges: Directly connect LANs
- Remote bridges: Can be used to create a wide area network (WAN) link between LANs. Remote bridges, where the connecting link is slower than the end networks, largely have been replaced with routers.
- Wireless bridges: Can be used to join LANs or connect remote stations to LANs.

Switches

A network switch is a device that forwards and filters OSI layer 2 datagrams (chunks of data communication) between ports (connected cables) based on the MAC addresses in the packets.[17] A switch is distinct from a hub in that it only forwards the frames to the ports involved in the communication rather than all ports connected. A switch breaks the collision domain but represents itself as a broadcast domain. Switches make forwarding decisions of frames on the basis of MAC addresses. A switch normally has numerous ports, facilitating a star topology for devices, and cascading additional switches.[18] Some switches are capable of routing based on Layer 3 addressing or additional logical levels; these are called multi-layer switches. The term *switch* is used loosely in marketing to encompass devices including routers and bridges, as well as devices that may distribute traffic on load or by application content (e.g., a Web URL identifier).

Routers

A router is an internetworking device that forwards packets between networks by processing information found in the datagram or packet (Internet protocol information from Layer 3 of the OSI Model). In many situations, this information is processed in conjunction with the routing table (also known as forwarding table). Routers use routing tables to determine what interface to forward packets (this can include the "null" also known as the "black hole" interface because data can go into it, however, no further processing is done for said data).

Firewalls

A firewall is an important aspect of a network with respect to security. It typically rejects access requests from unsafe sources while allowing actions from recognized ones. The vital role firewalls play in network security grows in parallel with the constant increase in 'cyber' attacks for the purpose of stealing/corrupting data, planting viruses, etc.

Network performance

Network performance refers to the service quality of a telecommunications product as seen by the customer. It should not be seen merely as an attempt to get "more through" the network.

The following list gives examples of Network Performance measures for a circuit-switched network and one type of packet-switched network, viz. ATM:

- Circuit-switched networks: In circuit switched networks, network performance is synonymous with the grade of service. The number of rejected calls is a measure of how well the network is performing under heavy traffic loads.[19] Other types of performance measures can include noise, echo and so on.

- ATM: In an Asynchronous Transfer Mode (ATM) network, performance can be measured by line rate, quality of service (QoS), data throughput, connect time, stability, technology, modulation technique and modem enhancements.[20]

There are many different ways to measure the performance of a network, as each network is different in nature and design. Performance can also be modelled instead of measured; one example of this is using state transition diagrams to model queuing performance in a circuit-switched network. These diagrams allow the network planner to analyze how the network will perform in each state, ensuring that the network will be optimally designed.[21]

Network security

In the field of networking, the area of **network security**[22] consists of the provisions and policies adopted by the network administrator to prevent and monitor unauthorized access, misuse, modification, or denial of the computer network and network-accessible resources. Network security is the authorization of access to data in a network, which is controlled by the network administrator. Users are assigned an ID and password that allows them access to information and programs within their authority. Network Security covers a variety of computer networks, both public and private that are used in everyday jobs conducting transactions and communications among businesses, government agencies and individuals.

Network resilience

In computer networking: "**Resilience** is the ability to provide and maintain an acceptable level of service in the face of faults and challenges to normal operation."[23]

Views of networks

Users and network administrators typically have different views of their networks. Users can share printers and some servers from a workgroup, which usually means they are in the same geographic location and are on the same LAN, whereas a Network Administrator is responsible to keep that network up and running. A community of interest has less of a connection of being in a local area, and should be thought of as a set of arbitrarily located users who share a set of servers, and possibly also communicate via peer-to-peer technologies.

Network administrators can see networks from both physical and logical perspectives. The physical perspective involves geographic locations, physical cabling, and the network elements (e.g., routers, bridges and application layer gateways) that interconnect the physical media. Logical networks, called, in the TCP/IP architecture, subnets, map onto one or more physical media. For example, a common practice in a campus of buildings is to make a set of LAN cables in each building appear to be a common subnet, using virtual LAN (VLAN) technology.

Both users and administrators will be aware, to varying extents, of the trust and scope characteristics of a network. Again using TCP/IP architectural terminology, an intranet is a community of interest under private administration usually by an enterprise, and is only accessible by authorized users (e.g. employees).[24] Intranets do not have to be connected to the Internet, but generally have a limited connection. An extranet is an extension of an intranet that allows secure communications to users outside of the intranet (e.g. business partners, customers).[24]

Unofficially, the Internet is the set of users, enterprises, and content providers that are interconnected by Internet Service Providers (ISP). From an engineering viewpoint, the Internet is the set of subnets, and aggregates of subnets, which share the registered IP address space and exchange information about the reachability of those IP addresses using the Border Gateway Protocol. Typically, the human-readable names of servers are translated to IP addresses, transparently to users, via the directory function of the Domain Name System (DNS).

Over the Internet, there can be business-to-business (B2B), business-to-consumer (B2C) and consumer-to-consumer (C2C) communications. Especially when money or sensitive information is exchanged, the communications are apt to be **secured** by some form of communications security mechanism. Intranets and extranets can be securely superimposed onto the Internet, without any access by general Internet users and administrators, using secure Virtual Private Network (VPN) technology.

See also

- Comparison of network diagram software
- Network topology

References

[1] *Computer network definition* (http://www.atis.org/glossary/definition.aspx?id=6555), , retrieved 2011-11-12

[2] Michael A. Banks (2008). *On the way to the web: the secret history of the internet and its founders* (http://books.google.com/books?id=P9wbSjO9WMMC&pg=PA1). Apress. p. 1. ISBN 9781430208693. .

[3] Christos J. P. Moschovitis (1998). *History of the Internet: a chronology, 1843 to the present* (http://books.google.com/?id=Hu5SAAAAMAAJ&dq=intitle:"history+of+the+internet"+sage+sabre&q=sage+sabre's#search_anchor). ABC-CLIO. p. 36. ISBN 9781576071182. .

[4] Chris Sutton. "Internet Began 35 Years Ago at UCLA with First Message Ever Sent Between Two Computers" (http://web.archive.org/web/20080308120314/http://www.engineer.ucla.edu/stories/2004/Internet35.htm). *UCLA*. Archived from the original (http://www.engineer.ucla.edu/stories/2004/Internet35.htm) on March 8, 2008. .

[5] *Broadband Over Powerline* (http://www.arrl.org/broadband-over-powerline-bpl), The National Association for Amateur Radio, , retrieved 2011-11-12

[6] "The Likelihood and Extent of Radio Frequency Interference from In-Home PLT Devices" (http://stakeholders.ofcom.org.uk/binaries/ research/technology-research/pltreport.pdf). Ofcom. . Retrieved 18 June 2011.

[7] "Mobile Broadband Wireless connections (MBWA)" (http://grouper.ieee.org/groups/802/20/). . Retrieved 2011-11-12.

[8] Bergen Linux User Group's CPIP Implementation (http://www.blug.linux.no/rfc1149)

[9] A. Hooke (September 2000), *Interplanetary Internet* (http://www.ipnsig.org/reports/ISART9-2000.pdf), Third Annual International Symposium on Advanced Radio Technologies, , retrieved 2011-11-12

[10] Martin, Thomas. "Design Principles for DSL-Based Access Solutions" (http://www.gsi.dit.upm.es/~legf/Varios/XDSL_MARTI.PDF). . Retrieved 18 June 2011.

[11] "personal area network (PAN)" (http://searchmobilecomputing.techtarget.com/sDefinition/0,,sid40_gci546288,00.html). . Retrieved January 29, 2011.

[12] *New global standard for fully networked home* (http://www.itu.int/ITU-T/newslog/New+Global+Standard+For+Fully+Networked+ Home.aspx), ITU-T, 2008-12-12, , retrieved 2011-11-12

[13] *IEEE P802.3ba 40Gb/s and 100Gb/s Ethernet Task Force* (http://www.ieee802.org/3/ba/), , retrieved 2011-11-12

[14] D. Andersen; H. Balakrishnan; M. Kaashoek; R. Morris (10-2001), *Resilient Overlay Networks* (http://nms.lcs.mit.edu/papers/ ron-sosp2001.html)], *Association for Computing Machinery*, , retrieved 2011-11-12

[15] http://esm.cs.cmu.edu/

[16] http://standards.ieee.org/regauth/oui/oui.txt

[17] "Define switch." (http://www.webopedia.com/TERM/s/switch.html). www.webopedia.com. . Retrieved April 8, 2008.

[18] "Basic Components of a Local Area Network (LAN)" (http://networkbits.net/lan-components/local-area-network-lan-basic-components/). NetworkBits.net. . Retrieved April 8, 2008.

[19] *Teletraffic Engineering Handbook* (http://web.archive.org/web/20070111015452/http://oldwww.com.dtu.dk/teletraffic/handbook/ telenook.pdf), ITU-T Study Group 2, archived from the original (http://www.com.dtu.dk/teletraffic/handbook/telenook.pdf) on 2007-01-11,

[20] Telecommunications Magazine Online (http://www.telecommagazine.com), Americas January 2003, Issue Highlights, Online Exclusive: Broadband Access Maximum Performance, Retrieved on February 13, 2005.

[21] "State Transition Diagrams" (http://cne.gmu.edu/modules/os_perf/std.t.html). . Retrieved July 13, 2003.

[22] Simmonds, A; Sandilands, P; van Ekert, L (2004). "An Ontology for Network Security Attacks". *Lecture Notes in Computer Science*. Lecture Notes in Computer Science **3285**: 317–323. doi:10.1007/978-3-540-30176-9_41. ISBN 978-3-540-23659-7.

[23] "Definitions: Resilience" (http://wiki.ittc.ku.edu/resilinets_wiki/index.php/Definitions#Resilience). ResiliNets Research Initiative. . Retrieved 2011-11-12.

[24] RFC 2547

Further reading

- Shelly, Gary, et al. "Discovering Computers" 2003 Edition
- Cisco Systems, Inc., (2003, March 14). CCNA: network media types. Retrieved from ciscopress.com (http:// www.ciscopress.com/articles/article.asp?p=31276&rll=1)
- Wendell Odom,Rus Healy, Denise Donohue. (2010) CCIE Routing and Switching. Indianapolis, IN: Cisco Press
- Kurose James F and Keith W. Ross : Computer Networking: A Top-Down Approach Featuring the Internet, Pearson Education 2005.
- Andrew S. Tanenbaum, *Computer Networks*, Fourth Edition, Pearson Education 2006 (ISBN 0-13-349945-6).
- William Stallings, *Computer Networking with Internet Protocols and Technology*, Pearson Education 2004.
- Important publications in computer networks
- Vinton G. Cerf "Software: Global Infrastructure for the 21st Century" (http://www.cs.washington.edu/homes/ lazowska/cra/networks.html)
- Meyers, Mike, "Mike Meyers' Certification Passport: Network+" ISBN 0072253487"
- Odom, Wendall, "CCNA Certification Guide"
- Network Communication Architecture and Protocols: OSI Network Architecture 7 Layers Model

External links

- Easy Network Concepts (http://www.netfilter.org/documentation/HOWTO/networking-concepts-HOWTO.html) (Linux kernel specific)
- Computer Networks and Protocol (http://nsgn.net/osi_reference_model/) (Research document, 2006)
- Computer Networking Glossary (http://compnetworking.about.com/od/basicnetworkingconcepts/l/blglossary.htm)
- Networking (http://www.dmoz.org/Computers/Software/Networking//) at the Open Directory Project

Intrusion_detection_system

An **intrusion detection system (IDS)** is a device or software application that monitors network or system activities for malicious activities or policy violations and produces reports to a Management Station.[1] Some systems may attempt to stop an intrusion attempt but this is neither required nor expected of a monitoring system.[1] Intrusion detection and prevention systems (IDPS) are primarily focused on identifying possible incidents, logging information about them, and reporting attempts.[1] In addition, organizations use IDPSes for other purposes, such as identifying problems with security policies, documenting existing threats, and deterring individuals from violating security policies.[1] IDPSes have become a necessary addition to the security infrastructure of nearly every organization.[1]

IDPSes typically record information related to observed events, notify security administrators of important observed events, and produce reports.[1] Many IDPSes can also respond to a detected threat by attempting to prevent it from succeeding.[1] They use several response techniques, which involve the IDPS stopping the attack itself, changing the security environment (e.g., reconfiguring a firewall), or changing the attack's content.[1]

Terminology

- **Alert/Alarm:** A signal suggesting that a system has been or is being attacked.[2]
- **True Positive:** A legitimate attack which triggers an IDS to produce an alarm.[2]
- **False Positive:** An event signaling an IDS to produce an alarm when no attack has taken place.[2]
- **False Negative:** A failure of an IDS to detect an actual attack.[2]
- **True Negative:** When no attack has taken place and no alarm is raised.
- **Noise:** Data or interference that can trigger a false positive.[2]
- **Site policy:** Guidelines within an organization that control the rules and configurations of an IDS.[2]
- **Site policy awareness:** An IDS's ability to dynamically change its rules and configurations in response to changing environmental activity.[2]
- **Confidence value:** A value an organization places on an IDS based on past performance and analysis to help determine its ability to effectively identify an attack.[2]
- **Alarm filtering:** The process of categorizing attack alerts produced from an IDS in order to distinguish false positives from actual attacks.[2]
- **Attacker or Intruder:** An entity who tries to find a way to gain unauthorized access to information, inflict harm or engage in other malicious activities.
- **Masquerader:** A user who does not have the authority to a system, but tries to access the information as an authorized user. They are generally outside users.
- **Misfeasor:** They are commonly internal users and can be of two types:
  1. An authorized user with limited permissions.
  2. A user with full permissions and who misuses their powers.
- **Clandestine user:** A user who acts as a supervisor and tries to use his privileges so as to avoid being captured.

Types

For the purpose of dealing with IT, there are two main types of IDS:

Network intrusion detection system (NIDS)

> is an independent platform that identifies intrusions by examining network traffic and monitors multiple hosts. Network intrusion detection systems gain access to network traffic by connecting to a network hub, network switch configured for port mirroring, or network tap. In a NIDS, sensors are located at choke points in the network to be monitored, often in the demilitarized zone (DMZ) or at network borders. Sensors capture all network traffic and analyzes the content of individual packets for malicious traffic. An example of a NIDS is Snort.

Host-based intrusion detection system (HIDS)

> It consists of an agent on a host that identifies intrusions by analyzing system calls, application logs, file-system modifications (binaries, password files, capability databases, Access control lists, etc.) and other host activities and state. In a HIDS, sensors usually consist of a software agent. Some application-based IDS are also part of this category. Examples of HIDS are Tripwire and OSSEC.

Stack-based intrusion detection system (SIDS)

> This type of system consists of an evolution to the HIDS systems. The packets are examined as they go through the TCP/IP stack and, therefore, it is not necessary for them to work with the network interface in promiscuous mode. This fact makes its implementation to be dependent on the Operating System that is being used.

Intrusion detection systems can also be system-specific using custom tools and honeypots.

Passive and/or reactive systems

In a **passive system**, the intrusion detection system (IDS) sensor detects a potential security breach, logs the information and signals an alert on the console and or owner. In a **reactive system**, also known as an intrusion prevention system (IPS), the IPS auto-responds to the suspicious activity by resetting the connection or by reprogramming the firewall to block network traffic from the suspected malicious source. The term IDPS is commonly used where this can happen automatically or at the command of an operator; systems that both "detect" (alert) or "prevent."

Comparison with firewalls

Though they both relate to network security, an intrusion detection system (IDS) differs from a firewall in that a firewall looks outwardly for intrusions in order to stop them from happening. Firewalls limit access between networks to prevent intrusion and do not signal an attack from inside the network. An IDS evaluates a suspected intrusion once it has taken place and signals an alarm. An IDS also watches for attacks that originate from within a system. This is traditionally achieved by examining network communications, identifying heuristics and patterns (often known as signatures) of common computer attacks, and taking action to alert operators. A system that terminates connections is called an intrusion prevention system, and is another form of an application layer firewall.

Statistical anomaly and signature based IDSes

All Intrusion Detection Systems use one of two detection techniques:

Statistical anomaly-based IDS

A statistical anomaly-based IDS determines normal network activity like what sort of bandwidth is generally used, what protocols are used, what ports and devices generally connect to each other- and alert the administrator or user when traffic is detected which is anomalous(not normal).[2]

Signature-based IDS

Signature based IDS monitors packets in the Network and compares with pre-configured and pre-determined attack patterns known as signatures. The issue is that there will be lag between the new threat discovered and Signature being applied in IDS for detecting the threat. During this lag time your IDS will be unable to identify the threat.[2]

Limitations

* Noise can severely limit an Intrusion detection system's effectiveness. Bad packets generated from software bugs, corrupt DNS data, and local packets that escaped can create a significantly high false-alarm rate.[3]
* It is not uncommon for the number of real attacks to be far below the false-alarm rate. Real attacks are often so far below the false-alarm rate that they are often missed and ignored.[3]
* Many attacks are geared for specific versions of software that are usually outdated. A constantly changing library of signatures is needed to mitigate threats. Outdated signature databases can leave the IDS vulnerable to new strategies.[3]

Evasion techniques

Intrusion detection system evasion techniques bypass detection by creating different states on the IDS and on the targeted computer. The adversary accomplishes this by manipulating either the attack itself or the network traffic that contains the attack.

Development

One preliminary IDS concept consisted of a set of tools intended to help administrators review audit trails.[4] User access logs, file access logs, and system event logs are examples of audit trails.

Fred Cohen noted in 1984 (see Intrusion Detection) that it is impossible to detect an intrusion in every case and that the resources needed to detect intrusions grows with the amount of usage.

Dorothy E. Denning, assisted by Peter G. Neumann, published a model of an IDS in 1986 that formed the basis for many systems today.[5] Her model used statistics for anomaly detection, and resulted in an early IDS at SRI International named the Intrusion Detection Expert System (IDES), which ran on Sun workstations and could consider both user and network level data.[6] IDES had a dual approach with a rule-based Expert System to detect known types of intrusions plus a statistical anomaly detection component based on profiles of users, host systems, and target systems. Lunt proposed adding an Artificial neural network as a third component. She said all three components could then report to a resolver. SRI followed IDES in 1993 with the Next-generation Intrusion Detection Expert System (NIDES).[7]

The Multics intrusion detection and alerting system (MIDAS), an expert system using P-BEST and Lisp, was developed in 1988 based on the work of Denning and Neumann.[8] Haystack was also developed this year using statistics to reduce audit trails.[9]

Wisdom & Sense (W&S) was a statistics-based anomaly detector developed in 1989 at the Los Alamos National Laboratory.[10] W&S created rules based on statistical analysis, and then used those rules for anomaly detection.

In 1990, the Time-based Inductive Machine (TIM) did anomaly detection using inductive learning of sequential user patterns in Common Lisp on a VAX 3500 computer.[11] The Network Security Monitor (NSM) performed masking on access matrices for anomaly detection on a Sun-3/50 workstation.[12] The Information Security Officer's Assistant (ISOA) was a 1990 prototype that considered a variety of strategies including statistics, a profile checker, and an expert system.[13] ComputerWatch at AT&T Bell Labs used statistics and rules for audit data reduction and intrusion detection.[14]

Then, in 1991, researchers at the University of California, Davis created a prototype Distributed Intrusion Detection System (DIDS), which was also an expert system.[15] The Network Anomaly Detection and Intrusion Reporter (NADIR), also in 1991, was a prototype IDS developed at the Los Alamos National Laboratory's Integrated Computing Network (ICN), and was heavily influenced by the work of Denning and Lunt.[16] NADIR used a statistics-based anomaly detector and an expert system.

The Lawrence Berkeley National Laboratory announced Bro in 1998, which used its own rule language for packet analysis from libpcap data.[17] Network Flight Recorder (NFR) in 1999 also used libpcap.[18] APE was developed as a packet sniffer, also using libpcap, in November, 1998, and was renamed Snort one month later, and has since become the world's largest used IDS/IPS system with over 300,000 active users.[19]

The Audit Data Analysis and Mining (ADAM) IDS in 2001 used tcpdump to build profiles of rules for classifications.[20]

In 2003, Dr. Yongguang Zhang and Dr. Wenke Lee argue for the importance of IDS in networks with mobile nodes.[21]

See also

- Anomaly-based intrusion detection system
- Application protocol-based intrusion detection system (APIDS)
- Artificial immune system
- Autonomous Agents for Intrusion Detection
- Host-based intrusion detection system (HIDS)
- Intrusion prevention system (IPS)
- Network intrusion detection system (NIDS)
- Protocol-based intrusion detection system (PIDS)
- Security Management

Free Intrusion Detection Systems

- ACARM-ng
- AIDE
- Bro NIDS
- OSSEC HIDS
- Prelude Hybrid IDS
- Samhain [22]
- Snort
- Suricata

References

ⓒ This article incorporates public domain material from the National Institute of Standards and Technology document "Guide to Intrusion Detection and Prevention Systems, SP800-94" [23] by Karen Scarfone, Peter Mell (retrieved on 1 January 2010).

[1] Scarfone, Karen; Mell, Peter (February 2007). "Guide to Intrusion Detection and Prevention Systems (IDPS)" (http://csrc.ncsl.nist.gov/publications/nistpubs/800-94/SP800-94.pdf). *Computer Security Resource Center* <marque> *(National Institute of Standards and Technology) (800-94*</marque>*). . Retrieved 1 January 2010.*

[2] nitin.; Mattord, verma (2008). *Principles of Information Security.* Course Technology. pp. 290–301. ISBN 978-1-4239-0177-8.

[3] Anderson, Ross (2001). *Security Engineering: A Guide to Building Dependable Distributed Systems.* New York: John Wiley & Sons. pp. 387–388. ISBN 978-0-471-38922-4.

[4] Anderson, James P., "Computer Security Threat Monitoring and Surveillance," Washing, PA, James P. Anderson Co., 1980.

[5] Denning, Dorothy E., "An Intrusion Detection Model," Proceedings of the Seventh IEEE Symposium on Security and Privacy, May 1986, pages 119–131

[6] Lunt, Teresa F., "IDES: An Intelligent System for Detecting Intruders," Proceedings of the Symposium on Computer Security; Threats, and Countermeasures; Rome, Italy, November 22–23, 1990, pages 110–121.

[7] Lunt, Teresa F., "Detecting Intruders in Computer Systems," 1993 Conference on Auditing and Computer Technology, SRI International

[8] Sebring, Michael M., and Whitehurst, R. Alan., "Expert Systems in Intrusion Detection: A Case Study," The 11th National Computer Security Conference, October, 1988

[9] Smaha, Stephen E., "Haystack: An Intrusion Detection System," The Fourth Aerospace Computer Security Applications Conference, Orlando, FL, December, 1988

[10] Vaccaro, H.S., and Liepins, G.E., "Detection of Anomalous Computer Session Activity," The 1989 IEEE Symposium on Security and Privacy, May, 1989

[11] Teng, Henry S., Chen, Kaihu, and Lu, Stephen C-Y, "Adaptive Real-time Anomaly Detection Using Inductively Generated Sequential Patterns," 1990 IEEE Symposium on Security and Privacy

[12] Heberlein, L. Todd, Dias, Gihan V., Levitt, Karl N., Mukherjee, Biswanath, Wood, Jeff, and Wolber, David, "A Network Security Monitor," 1990 Symposium on Research in Security and Privacy, Oakland, CA, pages 296–304

[13] Winkeler, J.R., "A UNIX Prototype for Intrusion and Anomaly Detection in Secure Networks," The Thirteenth National Computer Security Conference, Washington, DC., pages 115–124, 1990

[14] Dowell, Cheri, and Ramstedt, Paul, "The ComputerWatch Data Reduction Tool," Proceedings of the 13th National Computer Security Conference, Washington, D.C., 1990

[15] Snapp, Steven R, Brentano, James, Dias, Gihan V., Goan, Terrance L., Heberlein, L. Todd, Ho, Che-Lin, Levitt, Karl N., Mukherjee, Biswanath, Smaha, Stephen E., Grance, Tim, Teal, Daniel M. and Mansur, Doug, "DIDS (Distributed Intrusion Detection System) -- Motivation, Architecture, and An Early Prototype," The 14th National Computer Security Conference, October, 1991, pages 167–176.

[16] Jackson, Kathleen, DuBois, David H., and Stallings, Cathy A., "A Phased Approach to Network Intrusion Detection," 14th National Computing Security Conference, 1991

[17] Paxson, Vern, "Bro: A System for Detecting Network Intruders in Real-Time," Proceedings of The 7th USENIX Security Symposium, San Antonio, TX, 1998

[18] Amoroso, Edward, "Intrusion Detection: An Introduction to Internet Surveillance, Correlation, Trace Back, Traps, and Response," Intrusion.Net Books, Sparta, New Jersey, 1999, ISBN 0-9666700-7-8

[19] Kohlenberg, Toby (Ed.), Alder, Raven, Carter, Dr. Everett F. (Skip), Jr., Esler, Joel., Foster, James C., Jonkman Marty, Raffael, and Poor, Mike, "Snort IDS and IPS Toolkit," Syngress, 2007, ISBN 978-1-59749-099-3

[20] Barbara, Daniel, Couto, Julia, Jajodia, Sushil, Popyack, Leonard, and Wu, Ningning, "ADAM: Detecting Intrusions by Data Mining," Proceedings of the IEEE Workshop on Information Assurance and Security, West Point, NY, June 5–6, 2001

[21] Intrusion Detection Techniques for Mobile Wireless Networks, ACM WINET 2003 <http://www.cc.gatech.edu/~wenke/papers/winet03.pdf>

[22] http://www.la-samhna.de/samhain/

[23] http://csrc.ncsl.nist.gov/publications/nistpubs/800-94/SP800-94.pdf

Further reading

* Scarfone, Karen; Mell, Peter (February 2007). "Guide to Intrusion Detection and Prevention Systems (IDPS)" (http://csrc.ncsl.nist.gov/publications/nistpubs/800-94/SP800-94.pdf). *Computer Security Resource Center* (National Institute of Standards and Technology) (800-94). Retrieved 1 January 2010.
* "Intrusion Detection/Prevention Systems classification tree" (http://ipsec.pl/intrusion-detection/prevention-systems-classification-tree.html). IPsec.pl. Retrieved 30 July 2010.
* Singh, Abhishek; Lambert, Scott; Williams, Jeff. "Evasions In Intrusion Prevention Detection Systems" (http://www.virusbtn.com/virusbulletin/archive/2010/04/vb201004-evasions-in-IPS-IDS). Virus Bulletin. Retrieved April 2010.
* Bezroukov, Nikolai (11 December 2008). "Architectural Issues of Intrusion Detection Infrastructure in Large Enterprises (Revision 0.82)" (http://www.softpanorama.org/Articles/architectural_issues_of_intrusion_detection_infrastructure.shtml). Softpanorama. Retrieved 30 July 2010.

External links

* Intrusion Detection Systems (http://www.dmoz.org/Computers/Security/Intrusion_Detection_Systems/) at the Open Directory Project

Digital_evidence

Digital evidence or **electronic evidence** is any probative information stored or transmitted in digital form that a party to a court case may use at trial.[1] Before accepting digital evidence a court will determine if the evidence is relevant, whether it is authentic, if it is hearsay and whether a copy is acceptable or the original is required.[1]

The use of digital evidence has increased in the past few decades as courts have allowed the use of e-mails, digital photographs, ATM transaction logs, word processing documents, instant message histories, files saved from accounting programs, spreadsheets, internet browser histories, databases, the contents of computer memory, computer backups, computer printouts, Global Positioning System tracks, logs from a hotel's electronic door locks, and digital video or audio files.[2]

Many courts in the United States have applied the Federal Rules of Evidence to digital evidence in a similar way to traditional documents, although some have noted important differences. For example, that digital evidence tends to be more voluminous, more difficult to destroy, easily modified, easily duplicated, potentially more expressive, and more readily available. As such, some courts have sometimes treated digital evidence differently for purposes of authentication, hearsay, the best evidence rule, and privilege. In December 2006, strict new rules were enacted within the Federal Rules of Civil Procedure requiring the preservation and disclosure of electronically stored evidence. Digital evidence is often attacked for its authenticity due to the ease with which it can be modified, although courts are beginning to reject this argument without proof of tampering.[3]

Admissibility

Digital evidence is often ruled inadmissible by courts because it was obtained without authorization.[1] In most jurisdictions a warrant is required to seize and investigate digital devices. In a digital investigation this can present problems where, for example, evidence of other crimes are identified while investigating another. During a 1999 investigation into online harassment by Keith Schroeder investigators found pornographic images of children on his computer. A second warrant had to be obtained before the evidence could be used to charge Schroeder.[1] [4]

Authentication

As with any evidence, the proponent of digital evidence must lay the proper foundation. Courts largely concerned themselves with the reliability of such digital evidence.[3] As such, early court decisions required that authentication called "for a more comprehensive foundation." US v. Scholle, 553 F.2d 1109 (8th Cir. 1976). As courts became more familiar with digital documents, they backed away from the higher standard and have since held that "computer data compilations... should be treated as any other record." US v. Vela, 673 F.2d 86, 90 (5th Cir. 1982).

A common attack on digital evidence is that digital media can be easily altered. However, in 2002 a US court ruled that "the fact that it is possible to alter data contained in a computer is plainly insufficient to establish untrustworthiness" (US v. Bonallo, 858 F. 2d 1427 - 1988 - Court of Appeals, 9th).[1] [5]

Nevertheless, the "more comprehensive" foundation required by *Scholle* remains good practice. The American Law Reports lists a number ways to establish the comprehensive foundation. It suggests that the proponent demonstrate "the reliability of the computer equipment", "the manner in which the basic data was initially entered", "the measures taken to insure the accuracy of the data as entered", "the method of storing the data and the precautions taken to prevent its loss", "the reliability of the computer programs used to process the data", and "the measures taken to verify the accuracy of the program". 7 American Law Reports 4th, 8, 2b.

UK ACPO guidelines

In the United Kingdom examiners usually follow guidelines issued by the Association of Chief Police Officers (ACPO) for the authentication and integrity of evidence.[6] [7] The guidelines consist of four principles:

1. No action taken by law enforcement agencies or their agents should change data held on a computer or storage media which may subsequently be relied upon in court.
2. In exceptional circumstances, where a person finds it necessary to access original data held on a computer or on storage media, that person must be competent to do so and be able to give evidence explaining the relevance and the implications of their actions.
3. An audit trail or other record of all processes applied to computer based electronic evidence should be created and preserved. An independent third party should be able to examine those processes and achieve the same result.
4. The person in charge of the investigation (the case officer) has overall responsibility for ensuring that the law and these principles are adhered to.

These guidelines are widely accepted in courts of England and Scotland, but they do not constitute a legal requirement and their use is voluntary.

Best evidence rule

Digital evidence is almost never in a format readable by humans, requiring additional steps to include digital documents as evidence (i.e. printing out the material). It has been argued that this change of format may mean digital evidence does not qualify under the "best evidence rule".[3] However, the "Federal Rules of Evidence" rule 1001(3) states "if data are stored in a computer..., any printout or other output readable by sight, shown to reflect the data accurately, is an 'original.'"[8]

Commonly courts do not bar printouts under the best evidence rule. In *Aguimatang v. California State Lottery*, the court gave near *per se* treatment to the admissibility of digital evidence stating "the computer printout does not violate the best evidence rule, because a computer printout is considered an 'original.'" 234 Cal. App. 3d 769, 798.

Hearsay

Very often an opponent to digital evidence will object to its admission as hearsay. Like documentary evidence, not all digital evidence is hearsay.

First, there is some digital evidence which is not hearsay at all. Hearsay is a "statement, other than one made by the declarant while testifying at the trial... offered in evidence to prove the truth of the matter asserted." A declarant is a person. Therefore, courts have held that digital evidence is not hearsay when it is "the by-product of a machine operation which uses for its input 'statements' entered into the machine" and was "was generated solely by the electrical and mechanical operations of the computer and telephone equipment." *State v. Armstead*, 432 So.2d 837, 839 (La. 1983).

Moreover, where the evidence is not offered to prove the truth of the statements, digital evidence is not hearsay. This is the case, for example, with logs of chatroom conversations. While a chatroom log may contain many out of court statements, which would otherwise be hearsay, they may be used for other purposes, including as a party admission. *US v. Simpson*, 152 F.3s 1241 (10th Cir. 1998).

Second, hearsay recognizes a number of exceptions. Most frequently, proponents of digital evidence seek admission under the business records exception. This perhaps is because the definition of business records includes a "data compilation." FRE 803(6). However, obviously not every piece of digital evidence is a business record. Such reliance on the business records exception has had bad results for its proponents. In *Monotype Corp. PLC v. International Typeface Corp*, the plaintiffs relied on the business records exception to attempt to admit two e-mails as evidence that the defendants had infringed their copyright only to have it excluded by the court. 43 F.3d 443 (9th Cir. 1994). The court noted that the e-mail was not created "in the regular course of [the third party's] business."

Other proponents have had success with the public records exception, excited utterance, Present sense impression, and the FRE 807—the catch-all. Where digital evidence does not meet one of the other exceptions but has "equivalent circumstantial guarantees of trustworthiness" that hearsay seeks to protect against, a court may apply the catch-all.

References

[1] Casey, Eoghan (2004). *Digital Evidence and Computer Crime, Second Edition* (http://books.google.co.uk/books?id=Xo8GMt_AbQsC& hl=en&dq=Digital Evidence and Computer Crime, Second Edition&ei=it1XTMncCMm44gbC_qyFBw&sa=X&oi=book_result& ct=result&resnum=1&ved=0CDQQ6AEwAA). Elsevier. ISBN 0-12-163104-4. .

[2] Various (2009). Eoghan Casey. ed. *Handbook of Digital Forensics and Investigation* (http://books.google.co.uk/ books?id=xNjsDprqtUYC). Academic Press. pp. 567. ISBN 0123742676. . Retrieved 2 September 2010.

[3] Daniel J. Ryan; Gal Shpantzer. "Legal Aspects of Digital Forensics" (http://euro.ecom.cmu.edu/program/law/08-732/Evidence/ RyanShpantzer.pdf). . Retrieved 31 August 2010.

[4] "State v. Schroeder, 613 NW 2d 911 - Wis: Court of Appeals 2000" (http://scholar.google.co.uk/ scholar_case?case=6657201255979914796&q=Wisconsin+v+Schroeder&hl=en&as_sdt=2002&as_ylo=1998&as_yhi=2000). 2000. .

[5] "US v. Bonallo" (http://scholar.google.co.uk/scholar_case?case=17436631095971908840&q=US+v.+Bonallo&hl=en&as_sdt=2002& as_vis=1). Court of Appeals, 9th Circuit. 1988. . Retrieved 1 September 2010.

[6] Pollitt, MM. "Report on digital evidence" (http://citeseerx.ist.psu.edu/viewdoc/download?doi=10.1.1.80.1663&rep=rep1&type=pdf). . Retrieved 24 July 2010.

[7] "ACPO Good Practice Guide for Computer-Based Evidence" (http://www.7safe.com/electronic_evidence/ ACPO_guidelines_computer_evidence_v4_web.pdf). ACPO. . Retrieved 24 July 2010.

[8] "Federal Rules of Evidence #702" (http://federalevidence.com/rules-of-evidence#Rule702). . Retrieved 23 August 2010.

Books

General:

- Stephen Mason, general editor, *Electronic Evidence* (http://www.stephenmason.eu/books/electronic-evidence/) (2nd edn, LexisNexis Butterworths, 2010 (http://rimer.butterworths.co.uk/webcat/enquiry/product/product_detail.asp?ProdID=4328)) covering Australia, Canada, England & Wales, Hong Kong, India, Ireland, New Zealand, Scotland, Singapore, South Africa, United States of America
- Stephen Mason, general editor, *International Electronic Evidence* (http://www.stephenmason.eu/books/international-electronic-evidence/), (British Institute of International and Comparative Law, 2008 (http://www.biicl.org/publications/view/-/id/121/)), covering Argentina, Austria, Belgium, Bulgaria, Croatia, Cyprus, Czech Republic, Denmark, Egypt, Estonia, Finland, France, Germany, Greece, Hungary, Iceland, Italy, Japan, Latvia, Lithuania, Luxembourg, Malta, Mexico, Netherlands, Norway, Poland, Romania, Russia, Slovakia, Slovenia, Spain, Sweden, Switzerland, Thailand and Turkey

United States of America on discovery and evidence:

- Michael R Arkfeld, *Arkfeld on Electronic Discovery and Evidence* (3rd edn, Lexis, 2011) Looseleaf
- Adam I. Cohen and David J. Lender, *Electronic Discovery: Law and Practice* (2nd end, Aspen Publishers, 2011) Looseleaf
- Jay E. Grenig, William C. Gleisner, Troy Larson and John L. Carroll, *eDiscovery & Digital Evidence* (2nd edn, Westlaw, 2011) Looseleaf
- Michele C.S. Lange and Kristen M. Nimsger, *Electronic Evidence and Discovery: What Every Lawyer Should Know* (2nd edn, American Bar Association, 2009)
- George L. Paul, *Foundations of Digital Evidence* (American Bar Association, 2008)
- Paul R. Rice, *Electronic Evidence - Law and Practice* (American Bar Association, 2005)

United States of America on discovery:

- Brent E. Kidwell, Matthew M. Neumeier and Brian D. Hansen, *Electronic Discovery* (Law Journal Press) Looseleaf
- Joan E. Feldman, *Essentials of Electronic Discovery: Finding and Using Cyber Evidence* (Glasser Legalworks, 2003)
- Sharon Nelson, Bruce A. Olson and John W. Simek, *The Electronic Evidence and Discovery Handbook* (American Bar Association, 2006)
- Ralph C. Losey, *e-Discovery: New Ideas, Case Law, Trends and Practices* (Westlaw, 2010)

United States of America on visual evidence:

- Gregory P. Joseph, *Modern Visual Evidence* (Law Journal Press) Looseleaf

Articles

- Jonathan D. Frieden and Leigh M. Murray, The Admissibility of Electronic Evidence Under the Federal Rules of Evidence (http://jolt.richmond.edu/v17i2/article5.pdf), XVII Rich. J.L. & Tech. 5 (2011).

See also

- Electronic discovery

External links

- Computer and Digital Forensics Discussion Forum (http://www.multimediaforensics.com)
- International Journal of Digital Evidence (http://www.ijde.org/) (IJDE)
- International Organization on Computer Evidence (http://www.ioce.org/) (IOCE)

- Scientific Group on Digital Evidence (http://ncfs.org/swgde/index.html)
- Digital Evidence: Standards and Principles (http://www.fbi.gov/hq/lab/fsc/backissu/april2000/swgde.htm)
- The Digital Evidence in the Information Era (http://www.crime-research.org/articles/chawki1/)
- Forensic IT group of ENFSI (http://www.enfsi.org)
- Digital Evidence and Electronic Signature Law Review (http://wwww.deaeslr.org/)

Computer_forensics

Computer forensics (sometimes known as **computer forensic science**[1]) is a branch of digital forensic science pertaining to legal evidence found in computers and digital storage media. The goal of computer forensics is to examine digital media in a forensically sound manner with the aim of identifying, preserving, recovering, analyzing and presenting facts and opinions about the information.

Although it is most often associated with the investigation of a wide variety of computer crime, computer forensics may also be used in civil proceedings. The discipline involves similar techniques and principles to data recovery, but with additional guidelines and practices designed to create a legal audit trail.

Computer forensics analysis is not limited only to computer media

Evidence from computer forensics investigations is usually subjected to the same guidelines and practices of other digital evidence. It has been used in a number of high profile cases and is becoming widely accepted as reliable within US and European court systems.

Overview

In the early 1980s personal computers became more accessible to consumers leading to their increased use in criminal activity (for example, to help commit fraud). At the same time, several new "computer crimes" were recognized (such as hacking). The discipline of computer forensics emerged during this time as a method to recover and investigate digital evidence for use in court. Since then computer crime and computer related crime has grown exponentially, and even has jumped 67% between 2002 and 2003.[2] Today it is used to investigate a wide variety of crime, including child pornography, fraud, cyberstalking, murder and rape. The discipline also features in civil proceedings as a form of information gathering (for example, Electronic discovery)

Forensic techniques and expert knowledge are used to explain the current state of a *digital artifact*; such as a computer system, storage medium (e.g. hard disk or CD-ROM), an electronic document (e.g. an email message or JPEG image).[3] The scope of a forensic analysis can vary from simple information retrieval to reconstructing a series of events. In a 2002 book *Computer Forensics* authors Kruse and Heiser define computer forensics as involving "the preservation, identification, extraction, documentation and interpretation of computer data".[4] They go on to describe the discipline as "more of an art than a science", indicating that forensic methodology is backed by flexibility and extensive domain knowledge. However, while several methods can be used to extract evidence from a given computer the strategies used by law enforcement are fairly rigid and lacking the flexibility found in the civilian world.[5]

Use as evidence

In court, computer forensic evidence is subject to the usual requirements for digital evidence. This requires that information be authentic, reliably obtained, and admissible. Different countries have specific guidelines and practices for evidence recovery. In the United Kingdom, examiners often follow Association of Chief Police Officers guidelines that help ensure the authenticity and integrity of evidence. While voluntary, the guidelines are widely accepted in courts in Wales, England, and Scotland.

Computer forensics has been used as evidence in criminal law since the mid 1980s, some notable examples include:[6]

BTK Killer

> Dennis Rader was convicted of a string of serial killings that occurred over a period of sixteen years. Towards the end of this period, Rader sent letters to the police on a floppy disk. Metadata within the documents implicated an author named "Dennis" at "Christ Lutheran Church"; this evidence helped lead to Rader's arrest.

Joseph E. Duncan III

> A spreadsheet recovered from Duncan's computer contained evidence that showed him planning his crimes. Prosecutors used this to show premeditation and secure the death penalty.[7]

Sharon Lopatka

> Hundreds of emails on Lopatka's computer lead investigators to her killer, Robert Glass.[6]

Corcoran Group

> This case confirmed parties' duties to preserve digital evidence when litigation has commenced or is reasonably anticipated. Hard drives were analyzed by a computer forensics expert, who could not find relevant e-mails the Defendants should have had. Though the expert found no evidence of deletion on the hard drives, evidence came out that the defendants were found to have intentionally destroyed emails, and misled and failed to disclose material facts to the plaintiffs and the court.

Dr. Conrad Murray

Dr. Conrad Murray, the doctor of the deceased Micheal Jackson, was convicted partially by digital evidence on his computer. This evidence included medical documentation showing lethal amounts of propofol.

Forensic process

Computer forensic investigations usually follow the standard digital forensic process (acquisition, analysis and reporting).[6] Investigations are performed on static data (i.e. acquired images) rather than "live" systems. This is a change from early forensic practices where a lack of specialist tools led to investigators commonly working on live data.

Techniques

A number of techniques are used during computer forensics investigations.

A portable Tableau write-blocker attached to a Hard Drive

Cross-drive analysis

> A forensic technique that correlates information found on multiple hard drives. The process, still being researched, can be used to identify social networks and for perform anomaly detection.[8] [9]

Live analysis

The examination of computers from within the operating system using custom forensics or existing sysadmin tools to extract evidence. The practice is useful when dealing with Encrypting File Systems, for example, where the encryption keys may be collected and, in some instances, the logical hard drive volume may be imaged (known as a live acquisition) before the computer is shut down.

Deleted files

A common technique used in computer forensics is the recovery of deleted files. Modern forensic software have their own tools for recovering or carving out deleted data.[10] Most operating systems and file systems do not always erase physical file data, allowing investigators to reconstruct it from the physical disk sectors. File carving involves searching for known file headers within the disk image and reconstructing deleted materials.

Steganography

One of the techniques used to hide data is via steganography, the process of hiding data inside of a picture or digital image. This process is often used to hide pornographic images of children as well as information that a given criminal does not want to have discovered. Computer forensics professionals can fight this by looking at the hash of the file and comparing it to the original image (if available.) While the image appears exactly the same, the hash changes as the data changes.[11]

Volatile data

When seizing evidence, if the machine is still active, any information stored solely in RAM that is not recovered before powering down may be lost.[7] One application of "live analysis" is to recover RAM data (for example, using Microsoft's COFEE tool, windd, WindowsSCOPE) prior to removing an exhibit.

RAM can be analyzed for prior content after power loss, because the electrical charge stored in the memory cells takes time to dissipate, an effect exploited by the cold boot attack. The length of time that data is recoverable is increased by low temperatures and higher cell voltages. Holding unpowered RAM below −60 °C helps preserve residual data by an order of magnitude, improving the chances of successful recovery. However, it can be impractical to do this during a field examination.[12]

Some of the tools needed to extract volatile data, however, require that a computer be in a forensic lab, both to maintain a legitimate chain of evidence, and to facilitate work on the machine. If necessary, law enforcement applies techniques to move a live, running desktop computer. These include a mouse jiggler, which moves the mouse rapidly in small movements and prevents the computer from going to sleep accidentally. Usually, an uninterruptible power supply (UPS) provides power during transit.

However, one of the easiest ways to capture data is by actually saving the RAM data to disk. Various file systems that have journaling features such as NTFS and ReiserFS keep a large portion of the RAM data on the main storage media during operation, and these page files can be reassembled to reconstruct what was in RAM at that time.[13]

Analysis tools

A number of open source and commercial tools exist for computer forensics investigation. Typical forensic analysis includes a manual review of material on the media, reviewing the Windows registry for suspect information, discovering and cracking passwords, keyword searches for topics related to the crime, and extracting e-mail and pictures for review.[6]

Certifications

There are several computer forensics certifications available, such as the ISFCE Certified Computer Examiner [14] and IACRB Certified Computer Forensics Examiner [15].

IACIS [16] (the International Association of Computer Investigative Specialists) offers the Certified Computer Forensic Examiner (CFCE) program.

Financial Forensics

Financial Forensics is a field fast catching up for Financial Fraud Investigators investigating Frauds. New tools and techniques are being developed and adopted. Nevertheless older methods and methodologies are being extensively used to trace redflags. Among them, the most commonly used technique is Benford's Law. Further specialized software tools and applications are being developed to do Financial Forensics on databases. Actimize and Memento are examples of them.

See also

- Counter forensics
- Cryptanalysis
- Data remanence
- Disk encryption
- Encryption
- Hidden file and hidden directory
- Information technology audit
- MAC times
- Steganalysis
- United States v. Arnold

References

[1] Michael G. Noblett; Mark M. Pollitt, Lawrence A. Presley (October 2000). "Recovering and examining computer forensic evidence" (http:// www.fbi.gov/about-us/lab/forensic-science-communications/fsc/oct2000/computer.htm). . Retrieved 26 July 2010.

[2] Leigland, R (September 2004). "A Formalization of Digital Forensics" (http://www.utica.edu/academic/institutes/ecii/publications/ articles/A0B8472C-D1D2-8F98-8F7597844CF74DF8.pdf). .

[3] A Yasinsac; RF Erbacher, DG Marks, MM Pollitt (2003). "Computer forensics education" (http://citeseerx.ist.psu.edu/viewdoc/ download?doi=10.1.1.1.9510&rep=rep1&type=pdf). IEEE Security & Privacy. . Retrieved 26 July 2010.

[4] Warren G. Kruse; Jay G. Heiser (2002). *Computer forensics: incident response essentials* (http://books.google.com/ books?id=nNpQAAAAMAAJ). Addison-Wesley. pp. 392. ISBN 0-201-70719-5. . Retrieved 6 December 2010.

[5] Gunsch, G (August 2002). "An Examination of Digital Forensic Models" (http://www.utica.edu/academic/institutes/ecii/publications/ articles/A04A40DC-A6F6-F2C1-98F94F16AF57232D.pdf). .

[6] Casey, Eoghan (2004). *Digital Evidence and Computer Crime, Second Edition* (http://books.google.com/?id=Xo8GMt_AbQsC& dq=Digital Evidence and Computer Crime, Second Edition). Elsevier. ISBN 0-12-163104-4. .

[7] Various (2009). Eoghan Casey. ed. *Handbook of Digital Forensics and Investigation* (http://books.google.co.uk/ books?id=xNjsDprqtUYC). Academic Press. pp. 567. ISBN 0-12-374267-6. . Retrieved 27 August 2010.

[8] Garfinkel, S. (August 2006). "Forensic Feature Extraction and Cross-Drive Analysis" (http://www.simson.net/clips/academic/2006. DFRWS.pdf). .

[9] "EXP-SA: Prediction and Detection of Network Membership through Automated Hard Drive Analysis" (http://www.nsf.gov/awardsearch/ showAward.do?AwardNumber=0730389). .

[10] Aaron Phillip; David Cowen, Chris Davis (2009). *Hacking Exposed: Computer Forensics* (http://books.google.co.uk/ books?id=yMdNrgSBUq0C). McGraw Hill Professional. pp. 544. ISBN 0-07-162677-8. . Retrieved 27 August 2010.

[11] Dunbar, B (January 2001). "A detailed look at Steganographic Techniques and their use in an Open-Systems Environment" (http://www. sans.org/reading_room/whitepapers/covert/detailed-steganographic-techniques-open-systems-environment_677). .

[12] J. Alex Halderman, Seth D. Schoen, Nadia Heninger, William Clarkson, William Paul, Joseph A. Calandrino, Ariel J. Feldman, Jacob Appelbaum, and Edward W. Felten (2008-02-21). *Lest We Remember: Cold Boot Attacks on Encryption Keys* (http://citp.princeton.edu/ memory/). Princeton University. . Retrieved 2009-11-20.

[13] Geiger, M (March 2005). "Evaluating Commercial Counter-Forensic Tools" (http://www.dfrws.org/2005/proceedings/ geiger_couterforensics.pdf). .

[14] http://www.isfce.com/

[15] http://www.iacertification.org/ccfe_certified_computer_forensics_examiner.html

[16] https://www.iacis.com/

Further reading

- A Practice Guide to Computer Forensics, First Edition (Paperback) by David Benton (Author), Frank Grindstaff (Author)
- Casey, Eoghan; Stellatos, Gerasimos J. (2008). "The impact of full disk encryption on digital forensics". *Operating Systems Review* **42** (3): 93–98. doi:10.1145/1368506.1368519.
- YiZhen Huang and YangJing Long (2008). "Demosaicking recognition with applications in digital photo authentication based on a quadratic pixel correlation model" (http://pages.cs.wisc.edu/~huangyz/ cvpr08_Huang.pdf). *Proc. IEEE Conference on Computer Vision and Pattern Recognition*: 1–8.
- Incident Response and Computer Forensics, Second Edition (Paperback) by Chris Prosise (Author), Kevin Mandia (Author), Matt Pepe (Author) "Truth is stranger than fiction..." (more)
- Ross, S. and Gow, A. (1999). *Digital archaeology? Rescuing Neglected or Damaged Data Resources* (http:// www.ukoln.ac.uk/services/elib/papers/supporting/pdf/p2.pdf). Bristol & London: British Library and Joint Information Systems Committee. ISBN 1-900508-51-6.
- George M. Mohay (2003). *Computer and intrusion forensics* (http://books.google.com/ books?id=z4GLgpwsYrkC). Artech House. pp. 395. ISBN 1-58053-369-8.

Related journals

- *IEEE Transactions on Information Forensics and Security* (http://ieeexplore.ieee.org/xpl/RecentIssue. jsp?punumber=10206)
- *Journal of Digital Forensics, Security and Law* (http://www.jdfsl.org)
- *International Journal of Digital Crime and Forensics* (http://www.dcs.warwick.ac.uk/~ctli/IJDCF.html)
- *Journal of Digital Investigation* (http://www.elsevier.com/wps/find/journaldescription.cws_home/702130/ description#description)
- *International Journal of Digital Evidence* (http://www.utica.edu/academic/institutes/ecii/ijde/)
- *International Journal of Forensic Computer Science* (http://www.ijofcs.org/)
- *Journal of Digital Forensic Practice* (http://www.tandf.co.uk/journals/titles/15567281.asp)
- *Cryptologia* (http://www.tandf.co.uk/journals/titles/01611194.asp)
- *Small Scale Digital Device Forensic Journal* (http://www.ssddfj.org)

External links

- US NIST Digital Data Acquisition Tool Specification (http://www.cftt.nist.gov/Pub-Draft-1-DDA-Require. pdf) (PDF)
- Forensics Wiki (http://www.forensicswiki.org), a Creative Commons wiki of computer forensics information.
- Computer Forensics World Forum (http://www.computerforensicsworld.com)
- Original Computer Forensics Wiki (http://computer-forensics.safemode.org/)
- Electronic Evidence Information Center (http://www.e-evidence.info)
- Forensic Focus (http://www.forensicfocus.com)
- Digital Forensic Research Workshop (DFRWS) (http://www.dfrws.org)
- Computer Forensic Whitepapers (SANS) (http://computer-forensics.sans.org/community/whitepapers)
- Forensic Science Information and Resources (http://www.forensicsciencenews.org)

Ethernet

Ethernet ◄) /'iːθərnɛt/ is a family of computer networking technologies for local area networks (LANs) commercially introduced in 1980. Standardized in IEEE 802.3, Ethernet has largely replaced competing wired LAN technologies. In the OSI reference system, Ethernet is at the Data Link layer.

Systems communicating over Ethernet divide a stream of data into individual packets called frames. Each frame contains source and destination addresses and error-checking data so that damaged data can be detected and re-transmitted.

The standards comprise several wiring and signaling variants of the OSI physical layer in use with Ethernet. The original 10BASE5 Ethernet used coaxial cable as a shared medium. Later the coaxial cables were replaced by twisted pair and fiber optic links in conjunction with hubs or switches. Data rates were periodically increased from the original 10 megabits per second, to 100 gigabits per second.

An 8P8C modular connector (often called RJ45) commonly used on cat 5 cables in Ethernet networks

Since its commercial release, Ethernet has retained a good degree of compatibility. Features such as the 48-bit MAC address and Ethernet frame format have influenced other networking protocols.

History

Ethernet was developed at Xerox PARC between 1973 and 1974.[1] [2] It was inspired by ALOHAnet, which Robert Metcalfe had studied as part of his PhD dissertation.[3] The idea was first documented in a memo that Metcalfe wrote on May 22, 1973.[1] [4] In 1975, Xerox filed a patent application listing Metcalfe, David Boggs, Chuck Thacker and Butler Lampson as inventors.[5] In 1976, after the system was deployed at PARC, Metcalfe and Boggs published a seminal paper.[6] [7]

Metcalfe left Xerox in June 1979 to form 3Com.[1] [8] He convinced Digital Equipment Corporation (DEC), Intel, and Xerox to work together to promote Ethernet as a standard. The so-called "DIX" standard, for "Digital/Intel/Xerox" specified 10 Mbit/s Ethernet, with 48-bit destination and source addresses and a global 16-bit Ethertype-type field. It was published on September 30, 1980 as "The Ethernet, A Local Area Network. Data Link Layer and Physical Layer Specifications".[9] Version 2 was published in November, 1982[10] and defines what has become known as Ethernet II. Formal standardization efforts proceeded at the same time.

Ethernet initially competed with two largely proprietary systems, Token Ring and Token Bus. Because Ethernet was able to adapt to market realities and shift to inexpensive and ubiquitous twisted pair wiring, these proprietary protocols soon found themselves competing in a market inundated by Ethernet products and by the end of the 1980s, Ethernet was clearly the dominant network technology.[1] In the process, 3Com became a major company. 3Com shipped its first 10 Mbit/s Ethernet 3C100 transceiver in March 1981, and that year started selling adapters for PDP-11s and VAXes, as well as Multibus-based Intel and Sun Microsystems computers.[11] :9 This was followed quickly by DEC's Unibus to Ethernet adapter, which DEC sold and used internally to build its own corporate network, which reached over 10,000 nodes by 1986, making it one of the largest computer networks in the world at that time.[12] An Ethernet adapter card for the IBM PC was released in 1982 and by 1985, 3Com had sold 100,000.[8]

Since then Ethernet technology has evolved to meet new bandwidth and market requirements.[13] In addition to computers, Ethernet is now used to interconnect appliances and other personal devices.[1] It is used in industrial applications and is quickly replacing legacy data transmission systems in the world's telecommunications networks.[14] By 2010, the market for Ethernet equipment amounted to over $16 billion per year.[15]

Standardization

Notwithstanding its technical merits, timely standardization was instrumental to the success of Ethernet. It required well-coordinated and partly competitive activities in several standardization bodies such as the IEEE, ECMA, IEC, and finally ISO.

In February 1980, the Institute of Electrical and Electronics Engineers (IEEE) started project 802 to standardize local area networks (LAN).[16] [8]

The "DIX-group" with Gary Robinson (DEC), Phil Arst (Intel), and Bob Printis (Xerox) submitted the so-called "Blue Book" CSMA/CD specification as a candidate for the LAN specification.[9] In addition to CSMA/CD, Token Ring (supported by IBM) and Token Bus (selected and henceforward supported by General Motors) were also considered as candidates for a LAN standard. Competing proposals and broad interest in the initiative led to strong disagreement over which technology to standardize. In December 1980, the group was split into three subgroups and standardization proceeded separate for each proposal.[8]

Delays in the standards process put at risk the market introduction of the Xerox Star workstation and 3Com's Ethernet LAN products. With such business implications in mind, David Liddle (General Manager, Xerox Office Systems) and Metcalfe (3Com) strongly supported a proposal of Fritz Röscheisen (Siemens Private Networks) for an alliance in the emerging office communication market, including Siemens' support for the international standardization of Ethernet (April 10, 1981). Ingrid Fromm, Siemens' representative to IEEE 802, quickly achieved broader support for Ethernet beyond IEEE by the establishment of a competing Task Group "Local Networks" within the European standards body ECMA TC24. As early as March 1982 ECMA TC24 with its corporate members reached agreement on a standard for CSMA/CD based on the IEEE 802 draft.[11] :8 Because the DIX proposal was most technically complete and because of the speedy action taken by ECMA which decisively contributed to the conciliation of opinions within IEEE, the IEEE 802.3 CSMA/CD standard was approved in December 1982.[8] IEEE published the 802.3 standard as a draft in 1983 and as a standard in 1985.

Approval of Ethernet on the international level was achieved by a similar, cross-partisan action with Fromm as liaison officer working to integrate International Electrotechnical Commission, TC83 and International Organization for Standardization (ISO) TC97SC6, and the ISO/IEEE 802/3 standard was approved in 1984.

Evolution

Ethernet evolved to include higher bandwidth, improved media access control methods, and different physical media. The coaxial cable was replaced with point-to-point links connected by Ethernet repeaters or switches to reduce installation costs, increase reliability, and improve management and troubleshooting. Many variants of Ethernet remain in common use.

Ethernet stations communicate by sending each other data packets: blocks of data individually sent and delivered. As with other IEEE 802 LANs, each Ethernet station is given a 48-bit MAC address. The MAC addresses are used to specify both the destination and the source of each data packet. Ethernet establishes link level connections, which can be defined using both the destination and source addresses. On reception of a transmission, the receiver uses the destination address to determine whether the transmission is relevant to the station or should be ignored. Network interfaces normally do not accept packets addressed to other Ethernet stations. Adapters come programmed with a globally unique address.[17] An Ethertype field in each frame is used by the operating system on the receiving station to select the appropriate protocol module (i.e. the Internet protocol module). Ethernet frames are said to be self-identifying, because of the frame type. Self-identifying frames make it possible to intermix multiple protocols on the same physical network and allow a single computer to use multiple protocols together.[18] Despite the evolution of Ethernet technology, all generations of Ethernet (excluding early experimental versions) use the same frame formats[19] (and hence the same interface for higher layers), and can be readily interconnected through bridging.

Due to the ubiquity of Ethernet, the ever-decreasing cost of the hardware needed to support it, and the reduced panel space needed by twisted pair Ethernet, most manufacturers now build Ethernet interfaces directly into PC motherboards, eliminating the need for installation of a separate network card.[20]

Shared media

Ethernet was originally based on the idea of computers communicating over a shared coaxial cable acting as a broadcast transmission medium. The methods used were similar to those used in radio systems,[21] with the common cable providing the communication channel likened to the *Luminiferous aether* in 19th century physics, and it was from this reference that the name "Ethernet" was derived.[22]

Original Ethernet's shared coaxial cable (the shared medium) traversed a building or campus to every attached machine. A scheme known as carrier sense multiple access with collision detection (CSMA/CD) governed the way the computers shared the channel. This scheme was simpler than the competing token ring or token bus technologies.[23] Computers were connected to an Attachment Unit Interface (AUI) transceiver, which was in turn connected to the cable (later with thin Ethernet the transceiver was integrated into the network adapter).

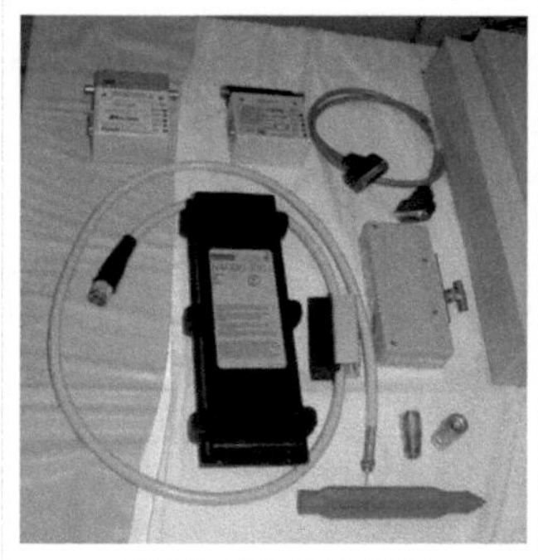
10BASE5 Ethernet equipment

While a simple passive wire was highly reliable for small networks, it was not reliable for large extended networks, where damage to the wire in a single place, or a single bad connector, could make the whole Ethernet segment unusable.[24]

Through the first half of the 1980s, Ethernet's 10BASE5 implementation used a coaxial cable 0.375 inches **(unknown operator: u'strong'** mm) in diameter, later called "thick Ethernet" or "thicknet". Its successor, 10BASE2, called "thin Ethernet" or "thinnet", used a cable similar to cable television cable of the era. The emphasis was on making installation of the cable easier and less costly.

Since all communications happen on the same wire, any information sent by one computer is received by all, even if that information is intended for just one destination.[25] The network interface card interrupts the CPU only when applicable packets are received: The card ignores information not addressed to it.[26] Use of a single cable also means that the bandwidth is shared, such that, for example, available bandwidth to each device is halved when two stations are simultaneously active.

Collisions corrupt transmitted data and require stations to retransmit. The lost data and retransmissions reduce throughput. In the worst case where multiple active hosts connected with maximum allowed cable length attempt to transmit many short frames, excessive collisions can reduce throughput dramatically. However, a Xerox report in 1980 studied performance of an existing Ethernet installation under both normal and artificially generated heavy load. The report claims that 98% throughput on the LAN was observed.[27] This is in contrast with token passing LANs (token ring, token bus), all of which suffer throughput degradation as each new node comes into the LAN, due to token waits. This report was controversial, as modeling showed that collision-based networks became unstable under loads as low as 40% of nominal capacity. Many early researchers failed to understand the subtleties of the CSMA/CD protocol and how important it was to get the details right, and were really modeling somewhat different networks (usually not as good as real Ethernet).[28]

Repeaters and hubs

For signal degradation and timing reasons, coaxial Ethernet segments had a restricted size. Somewhat larger networks could be built by using an Ethernet repeater. Early repeaters had only two ports, allowing, at most, a doubling of network size. Once repeaters with more than two ports became available, it was possible to wire the network in a star topology. Early experiments with star topologies (called "Fibernet") using optical fiber were published by 1978.[29]

A 1990s network interface card supporting both coaxial cable-based 10BASE2 (BNC connector, left) and twisted pair-based 10BASE-T (8P8C connector, right)

Shared cable Ethernet was always hard to install in offices because its bus topology was in conflict with the star topology cable plans designed into buildings for telephony. Modifying Ethernet to conform to twisted pair telephone wiring already installed in commercial buildings provided another opportunity to lower costs, expand the installed base, and leverage building design, and, thus, twisted-pair Ethernet was the next logical development in the mid-1980s.

Ethernet on unshielded twisted-pair cables (UTP) began with StarLAN at 1 Mbit/s in the mid-1980s. In 1987 SynOptics introduced the first twisted-pair Ethernet at 10 Mbit/s in a star-wired cabling topology with a central hub, later called LattisNet.[30] [31] [8] These evolved into 10BASE-T, which was designed for point-to-point links only, and all termination was built into the device. This changed repeaters from a specialist device used at the center of large networks to a device that every twisted pair-based network with more than two machines had to use. The tree structure that resulted from this made Ethernet networks easier to maintain by preventing most faults with one peer or its associated cable from affecting other devices on the network.

Despite the physical star topology and the presence of separate transmit and receive channels in the twisted pair and fiber media, repeater based Ethernet networks still use half-duplex and CSMA/CD, with only minimal activity by the repeater, primarily the Collision Enforcement signal, in dealing with packet collisions. Every packet is sent to every port on the repeater, so bandwidth and security problems are not addressed. The total throughput of the repeater is limited to that of a single link, and all links must operate at the same speed.

Bridging and switching

While repeaters could isolate some aspects of Ethernet segments, such as cable breakages, they still forwarded all traffic to all Ethernet devices. This created practical limits on how many machines could communicate on an Ethernet network. The entire network was one collision domain, and all hosts had to be able to detect collisions anywhere on the network. This limited the number of repeaters between the farthest nodes. Segments joined by repeaters had to all operate at the same speed, making phased-in upgrades impossible.

Patch cables with patch fields of two Ethernet switches

To alleviate these problems, bridging was created to communicate at the data link layer while isolating the physical layer. With bridging, only well-formed Ethernet packets are forwarded from one Ethernet segment to another; collisions and packet errors are isolated. Prior to learning of network devices on the different segments, Ethernet bridges (and switches) work somewhat like Ethernet repeaters, passing all traffic between segments. However, as the bridge learns the addresses associated with each port, it forwards network traffic only to the necessary segments, improving overall performance. Broadcast traffic is still forwarded to all network segments. Bridges also overcame the limits on total segments between two hosts and allowed the mixing of speeds, both of which are critical to deployment of Fast Ethernet.

In 1989, the networking company Kalpana introduced their EtherSwitch, the first Ethernet switch.[32] This worked somewhat differently from an Ethernet bridge, in that only the header of the incoming packet would be examined before it was either dropped or forwarded to another segment. This greatly reduced the forwarding latency and the processing load on the network device. One drawback of this cut-through switching method was that packets that had been corrupted would still be propagated through the network, so a jabbering station could continue to disrupt the entire network. The eventual remedy for this was a return to the original store and forward approach of bridging, where the packet would be read into a buffer on the switch in its entirety, verified against its checksum and then forwarded, but using more powerful application-specific integrated circuits. Hence, the bridging is then done in hardware, allowing packets to be forwarded at full wire speed.

When a twisted pair or fiber link segment is used and neither end is connected to a repeater, full-duplex Ethernet becomes possible over that segment. In full-duplex mode, both devices can transmit and receive to and from each other at the same time, and there is no collision domain. This doubles the aggregate bandwidth of the link and is sometimes advertised as double the link speed (e.g., 200 Mbit/s).[33] The elimination of the collision domain for these connections also means that all the link's bandwidth can be used by the two devices on that segment and that segment length is not limited by the need for correct collision detection.

Since packets are typically delivered only to the port they are intended for, traffic on a switched Ethernet is less public than on shared-medium Ethernet. Despite this, switched Ethernet should still be regarded as an insecure network technology, because it is easy to subvert switched Ethernet systems by means such as ARP spoofing and MAC flooding.

The bandwidth advantages, the slightly better isolation of devices from each other, the ability to easily mix different speeds of devices and the elimination of the chaining limits inherent in non-switched Ethernet have made switched Ethernet the dominant network technology.[34]

Advanced networking

Simple switched Ethernet networks, while a great improvement over repeater-based Ethernet, suffer from single points of failure, attacks that trick switches or hosts into sending data to a machine even if it is not intended for it, scalability and security issues with regard to broadcast radiation and multicast traffic, and bandwidth choke points where a lot of traffic is forced down a single link.

Advanced networking features in switches and routers combat these issues through means including spanning-tree protocol to maintain the active links of the network as a tree while allowing physical loops for redundancy, port security and protection features such as MAC lock down and broadcast radiation filtering, virtual LANs to keep different classes of users separate while using the same physical infrastructure, multilayer switching to route between different classes and link aggregation to add bandwidth to overloaded links and to provide some measure of redundancy.

A core Ethernet switch

Networking advances IEEE 802.1aq (SPB) include the use of the link-state routing protocol IS-IS to allow larger networks with shortest path routes between devices.

Varieties of Ethernet

The Ethernet physical layer evolved over a considerable time span and encompasses coaxial, twisted pair and fiber optic physical media interfaces and speeds from 10 Mbit to 100 Gbit. The most common forms used are 10BASE-T, 100BASE-TX, and 1000BASE-T. All three utilize twisted pair cables and 8P8C modular connectors. They run at 10 Mbit/s, 100 Mbit/s, and 1 Gbit/s, respectively. Fiber optic variants of Ethernet offer high performance, electrical isolation and distance (tens of kilometers with some versions). In general, network protocol stack software will work similarly on all varieties.

Ethernet frames

A data packet on the wire is called a frame. A frame begins with preamble and start frame delimiter, followed by an Ethernet header featuring source and destination MAC addresses. The middle section of the frame consists of payload data including any headers for other protocols (e.g., Internet Protocol) carried in the frame. The frame ends with a 32-bit cyclic redundancy check, which is used to detect corruption of data in transit.

Autonegotiation

Autonegotiation is the procedure by which two connected devices choose common transmission parameters, such as speed and duplex mode. Autonegotiation was first introduced as an optional feature for 100BASE-TX, but it is also backward compatible with 10BASE-T. Autonegotiation is mandatory for 1000BASE-T.

See also

- Gigabit Ethernet
- 10 Gigabit Ethernet
- 100 Gigabit Ethernet
- 5-4-3 rule
- AUI, GBIC, SFP, MII and PHY (chip)
- Chaosnet
- Ethernet crossover cable
- Fiber media converter
- Industrial Ethernet
- List of device bit rates
- Metro Ethernet
- Power over Ethernet
- Point-to-Point Protocol over Ethernet
- Wake-on-LAN

Notes

[1] *The History of Ethernet* (http://www.youtube.com/watch?v=g5MezxMcRmk). NetEvents.tv. 2006. . Retrieved September 10, 2011.

[2] "Ethernet Prototype Circuit Board" (http://americanhistory.si.edu/collections/object.cfm?key=35&objkey=96). Smithsonian National Museum of American History. 1973. . Retrieved September 2, 2007.

[3] Gerald W. Brock (September 25, 2003). *The Second Information Revolution*. Harvard University Press. p. 151. ISBN 0-674-01178-3.

[4] Mary Bellis. "Inventors of the Modern Computer" (http://inventors.about.com/library/weekly/aal11598.htm). About.com. . Retrieved September 10, 2011.

[5] U.S. Patent 4063220 (http://www.google.com/patents?vid=4063220) "Multipoint data communication system (with collision detection)"

[6] Robert Metcalfe; David Boggs (July 1976). "Ethernet: Distributed Packet Switching for Local Computer Networks" (http://www.acm.org/classics/apr96/). *Communications of the ACM* 19 (7): 395–405. doi:10.1145/360248.360253. .

[7] The experimental Ethernet described in the 1976 paper ran at 2.94 Mbit/s and had eight-bit destination and source address fields, so the original Ethernet addresses were not the MAC addresses they are today.John F. Shoch; Yogen K. Dalal; David D. Redell; Ronald C. Crane (August 1982). "Evolution of the Ethernet Local Computer Network" (http://ethernethistory.typepad.com/papers/EthernetEvolution.pdf). *IEEE Computer* 15 (8): 14–26. doi:10.1109/MC.1982.1654107. . By software convention, the 16 bits after the destination and source address fields specified a "packet type", but, as the paper says, "different protocols use disjoint sets of packet types". Thus the original packet types could vary within each different protocol. This is in contrast to the EtherType in the IEEE Ethernet standard, which specifies the protocol being used.

[8] Urd Von Burg; Martin Kenny (December 2003). "Sponsors, Communities, and Standards: Ethernet vs. Token Ring in the Local Area Networking Business" (http://hcd.ucdavis.edu/faculty/webpages/kenney/articles_files/Sponsors, Communities, and Standards: Ethernet vs.Token Ring in the Local Area Networking Business.pdf). Archived (http://www.webcitation.org/66LCgXKhx) from the original on 2012-03-21. .

[9] Digital Equipment Corporation, Intel Corporation and Xerox Corporation (30 September 1980), *The Ethernet, A Local Area Network. Data Link Layer and Physical Layer Specifications, Version 1.0* (http://ethernethistory.typepad.com/papers/EthernetSpec.pdf), Xerox Corporation, , retrieved 2011-12-10

[10] Digital Equipment Corporation, Intel Corporation and Xerox Corporation (November 1982), *The Ethernet, A Local Area Network. Data Link Layer and Physical Layer Specifications, Version 2.0* (http://decnet.ipv7.net/docs/dundas/aa-k759b-tk.pdf), Xerox Corporation, , retrieved 2011-12-10

[11] Robert Breyer & Sean Riley (1999). *Switched, Fast, and Gigabit Ethernet*. Macmillan. ISBN 1-57870-073-6.

[12] Jamie Parker Pearson (1992). *Digital at Work*. Digital Press. p. 163. ISBN 1-55558-092-0.

[13] Rick Merritt (December 20, 2010). *Shifts, growth ahead for 10G Ethernet* (http://www.eetimes.com/electronics-news/4211609/Shifts-growth-ahead-for-10G-Ethernet). E Times. . Retrieved September 10, 2011.

[14] "My oh My – Ethernet Growth Continues to Soar; Surpasses Legacy" (http://www.jaymiescotto.com/jsablog/2011/07/29/my-oh-my-ethernet-growth-continues-to-soar-surpasses-legacy/). Telecom News Now. July 29, 2011. . Retrieved September 10, 2011.

[15] Jim Duffy (February 22, 2010). *Cisco, Juniper, HP drive Ethernet switch market in Q4* (http://www.networkworld.com/news/2010/022210-ethernet-switch-market.html). Network World. . Retrieved September 10, 2011.

[16] Vic Hayes (August 27, 2001). "Letter to FCC" (http://www.ieeeusa.org/policy/policy/2001/01aug27IEEE802.pdf). . Retrieved October 22, 2010. "IEEE 802 has the basic charter to develop and maintain networking standards... IEEE 802 was formed in February 1980..."

[17] In some cases, the factory-assigned address can be overridden, either to avoid an address change when an adapter is replaced or to use locally administered addresses.

[18] Douglas E. Comer (2000). *Internetworking with TCP/IP – Principles, Protocols and Architecture* (4th ed.). Prentice Hall. ISBN 0-13-018380-6. 2.4.9 – Ethernet Hardware Addresses, p. 29, explains the filtering.

[19] Iljitsch van Beijnum. "Speed matters: how Ethernet went from 3Mbps to 100Gbps... and beyond" (http://arstechnica.com/gadgets/news/2011/07/ethernet-how-does-it-work.ars). Ars Technica. . Retrieved July 15, 2011. "All aspects of Ethernet were changed: its MAC procedure, the bit encoding, the wiring... only the packet format has remained the same."

[20] Geetaj Channana (November 1, 2004). "Motherboard Chipsets Roundup" (http://pcquest.ciol.com/content/search/showarticle.asp?artid=63428). PCQuest. . Retrieved October 22, 2010. "While comparing motherboards in the last issue we found that all motherboards support Ethernet connection on board."

[21] There are fundamental differences between wireless and wired shared-medium communications, such as the fact that it is much easier to detect collisions in a wired system than a wireless system.

[22] Charles E. Spurgeon (2000). *Ethernet: The Definitive Guide*. O'Reilly. ISBN 978-1-56592-660-8.

[23] In a CSMA/CD system packets must be large enough to guarantee that the leading edge of the propagating wave of the message got to all parts of the medium before the transmitter could stop transmitting, thus guaranteeing that collisions (two or more packets initiated within a window of time that forced them to overlap) would be discovered. Minimum packet size and the physical medium's total length were, thus, closely linked.

[24] Multipoint systems are also prone to strange failure modes when an electrical discontinuity reflects the signal in such a manner that some nodes would work properly, while others work slowly because of excessive retries or not at all. See standing wave for an explanation. These could be much more difficult to diagnose than a complete failure of the segment.

[25] This "one speaks, all listen" property is a security weakness of shared-medium Ethernet, since a node on an Ethernet network can eavesdrop on all traffic on the wire if it so chooses.

[26] Unless it is put into promiscuous mode.

[27] Shoch, John F. and Hupp, Jon A. (December 1980). "Measured performance of an Ethernet local network" (http://portal.acm.org/citation. cfm?doid=359038.359044#abstract). *Communications of the ACM* (ACM Press) **23** (12): 711–721. doi:10.1145/359038.359044. ISSN 0001-0782. .

[28] Boggs, D.R., Mogul, J.C., and Kent, C.A. (August 1988). "Measured capacity of an Ethernet: myths and reality" (http://portal.acm.org/ citation.cfm?doid=52325.52347#abstract). *ACM SIGCOMM Computer Communication Review* (ACM Press) **18** (4): 222–234. doi:10.1145/52325.52347. ISBN 0-89791-279-9. .

[29] Eric G. Rawson; Robert M. Metcalfe (July 1978). "Fibemet: Multimode Optical Fibers for Local Computer Networks" (http:// ethernethistory.typepad.com/papers/Fibernet.pdf). *IEEE transactions on communications* **26** (7): 983–990. doi:10.1109/TCOM.1978.1094189. . Retrieved June 11, 2011.

[30] Spurgeon, Charles E. (2000). *Ethernet; The Definitive Guide* (http://books.google.com/books?id=MRChaUQr0Q0C&pg=PA20& lpg=PA20&dq=synoptics+unshielded+twisted+pair&source=bl&ots=oF5HLbKhsN&sig=aw-dUL9TPoDSaZT0I5ztZvchmjE&hl=en& ei=jGSGTfDQNIqDgAex8InECA&sa=X&oi=book_result&ct=result&resnum=1&ved=0CCQQ6AEwADg8#v=onepage&q=synoptics& f=false). Nutshell Handbook. O'Reilly. p. 29. ISBN 1-56592-660-9. .

[31] Urs von Burg (2001). *The Triumph of Ethernet: technological communities and the battle for the LAN standard* (http://books.google.com/ books?id=ooBqdIXIqbwC&pg=PA175). Stanford University Press. p. 175. ISBN 0-8047-4094-1. .

[32] The term *switch* was invented by device manufacturers and does not appear in the 802.3 standard.

[33] This is misleading, as performance will double only if traffic patterns are symmetrical.

[34] "Token Ring-to-Ethernet Migration" (http://www.cisco.com/en/US/solutions/collateral/ns340/ns394/ns74/ns149/ net_business_benefit09186a00800c92b9_ps6600_Products_White_Paper.html). Cisco. . Retrieved October 22, 2010. "Respondents were first asked about their current and planned desktop LAN attachment standards. The results were clear—switched Fast Ethernet is the dominant choice for desktop connectivity to the network"

References

Further reading

- Digital Equipment Corporation, Intel Corporation, Xerox Corporation (September, 1980). *The Ethernet: A Local Area Network* (http://portal.acm.org/citation.cfm?id=1015591.1015594). — Version 1.0 of the DIX specification.
- "Internetworking Technology Handbook" (http://docwiki.cisco.com/wiki/Ethernet_Technologies). Cisco Systems. Retrieved April 11, 2011.

External links

- IEEE 802.3 Ethernet working group (http://www.ieee802.org/3/)
- IEEE 802.3-2008 standard (http://standards.ieee.org/getieee802/802.3.html)

Internet_Protocol

The **Internet Protocol** (**IP**) is the principal communications protocol used for relaying datagrams (also known as network packets) across an internetwork using the Internet Protocol Suite. Responsible for routing packets across network boundaries, it is the primary protocol that establishes the Internet.

IP is the primary protocol in the Internet Layer of the Internet Protocol Suite and has the task of delivering datagrams from the source host to the destination host solely based on the addresses. For this purpose, IP defines datagram structures that encapsulate the data to be delivered. It also defines addressing methods that are used to label the datagram source and destination.

Historically, IP was the connectionless datagram service in the original Transmission Control Program introduced by Vint Cerf and Bob Kahn in 1974, the other being the connection-oriented Transmission Control Protocol (TCP). The Internet Protocol Suite is therefore often referred to as TCP/IP.

The first major version of IP, Internet Protocol Version 4 (IPv4), is the dominant protocol of the internet. Its successor is Internet Protocol Version 6 (IPv6), which is increasing in use.

Function

The Internet Protocol is responsible for addressing hosts and routing datagrams (packets) from a source host to the destination host across one or more IP networks. For this purpose the Internet Protocol defines an addressing system that has two functions: identifying hosts and providing a logical location service. This is accomplished by defining standard datagrams and a standard addressing system.

Datagram construction

Each datagram has two components, a header and a payload. The IP header is tagged with the source IP address, destination IP address, and other meta-data needed to route and deliver the datagram. The payload is the data to be transported. This process of nesting data payloads in a packet with a header is called encapsulation.

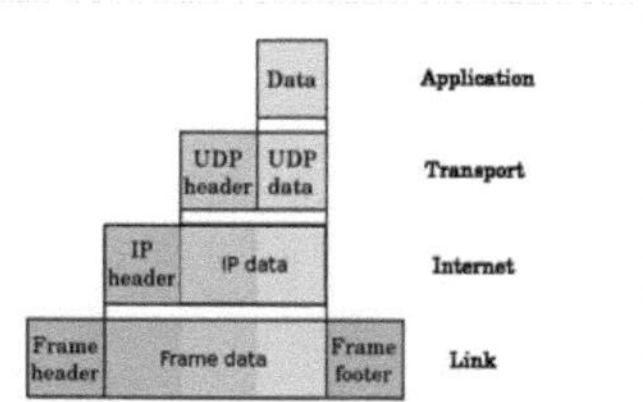

Sample encapsulation of application data from UDP to a Link protocol frame

IP addressing and routing

Perhaps the most complex aspects of IP are IP addressing and routing. Addressing refers to how end hosts are assigned IP addresses and how subnetworks of IP host addresses are divided and grouped. IP routing is performed by all hosts, but most importantly by routers, which typically use either interior gateway protocols (IGPs) or external gateway protocols (EGPs) to decide how to move datagrams among networks.

IP routing is also common in local networks. For example, Ethernet switches sold today support IP multicast.[1] These switches use IP addresses and Internet Group Management Protocol for control of the multicast routing but use MAC addresses for the actual routing.

Reliability

The design principles of the Internet protocols assume that the network infrastructure is inherently unreliable at any single network element or transmission medium and that it is dynamic in terms of availability of links and nodes. No central monitoring or performance measurement facility exists that tracks or maintains the state of the network. For the benefit of reducing network complexity, the intelligence in the network is purposely mostly located in the end nodes of each data transmission, cf. end-to-end principle. Routers in the transmission path simply forward packets to the next known local gateway matching the routing prefix for the destination address.

As a consequence of this design, the Internet Protocol only provides best effort delivery and its service is characterized as *unreliable*. In network architectural language it is a *connection-less* protocol, in contrast to so-called connection-oriented modes of transmission. The lack of reliability permits various error conditions, such as data corruption, packet loss and duplication, as well as out-of-order packet delivery. Since routing is dynamic for every packet and the network maintains no state of the path of prior packets, it is possible that some packets are routed on a longer path to their destination, resulting in improper sequencing at the receiver.

The only assistance that IPv4 provides regarding unreliability is to ensure that the IP packet header is error-free. A routing node calculates a checksum for a packet. If the checksum is bad, the routing node discards the packet. The routing node does not have to notify either end node, although the Internet Control Message Protocol (ICMP) allows such notification. In contrast, IPv6 abandons checksums in favor of faster routing.

Upper layer protocols are responsible for resolving reliability issues. For example, an upper layer protocol may cache data to make sure that it is in the correct order, before giving the data to an application.

In addition to issues of reliability, the dynamic nature and the diversity of the Internet and its components provide no guarantee that any particular path is actually capable of, or suitable for, performing the data transmission requested, even if the path is available and reliable. One of the technical constraints is the size of data packets allowed on a given link. An application must assure that it uses proper transmission characteristics. Some of this responsibility lies also in the upper layer protocols between application and IP. Facilities exist to examine the maximum transmission unit (MTU) size of the local link, as well as for the entire projected path to the destination when using IPv6. The IPv4 internetworking layer has the capability to automatically fragment the original datagram into smaller units for transmission. In this case, IP does provide re-ordering of fragments delivered out-of-order.[2]

Transmission Control Protocol (TCP) is an example of a protocol that will adjust its segment size to be smaller than the MTU. User Datagram Protocol (UDP) and Internet Control Message Protocol (ICMP) disregard MTU size, thereby forcing IP to fragment oversized datagrams.[3]

Version history

In May 1974, the Institute of Electrical and Electronic Engineers (IEEE) published a paper entitled "A Protocol for Packet Network Intercommunication."[4] The paper's authors, Vint Cerf and Bob Kahn, described an internetworking protocol for sharing resources using packet-switching among the nodes. A central control component of this model was the "Transmission Control Program" (TCP) that incorporated both connection-oriented links and datagram services between hosts. The monolithic Transmission Control Program was later divided into a modular architecture consisting of the Transmission Control Protocol at the connection-oriented layer and the Internet Protocol at the internetworking (datagram) layer. The model became known informally as TCP/IP, although formally referenced as the Internet Protocol Suite.

The Internet Protocol is one of the elements that define the Internet. The dominant internetworking protocol in the Internet Layer in use today is IPv4; the number 4 is the protocol version number carried in every IP datagram. IPv4 is described in RFC 791 (1981).

The successor to IPv4 is IPv6. Its most prominent modification from version 4 is the addressing system. IPv4 uses 32-bit addresses (c. 4 billion, or 4.3×10^9, addresses) while IPv6 uses 128-bit addresses (c. 340 undecillion, or

3.4×10^{38} addresses). Although adoption of IPv6 has been slow, as of June 2008, all United States government systems have demonstrated basic infrastructure support for IPv6 (if only at the backbone level).[5]

IP versions 0 to 3 were development versions of IPv4 and were used between 1977 and 1979. Version 5 was used by the Internet Stream Protocol, an experimental streaming protocol. Version numbers 6 through 9 were proposed for various protocol models designed to replace IPv4: SIPP (Simple Internet Protocol Plus, known now as IPv6), TP/IX (RFC 1475), PIP (RFC 1621) and TUBA (TCP and UDP with Bigger Addresses, RFC 1347).

Other protocol proposals named *IPv9* and *IPv8* briefly surfaced, but have no support.[6]

On April 1, 1994, the IETF published an April Fool's Day joke about IPv9.[7]

Vulnerabilities

The Internet Protocol is vulnerable to a variety of attacks. A thorough vulnerability assessment, along with proposed mitigations, was published in 2008,[8] and is currently being pursued within the IETF.[9]

See also

- Outline of the Internet
- List of Internet topics
- All IP
- ATM
- Connectionless protocol
- Flat IP
- Geolocation software
- IANA
- Internet
- Internet Protocol Suite
- Internet Stream Protocol
- ip - the ip structure for the C programming language
- IP address
- IP fragmentation
- IPv4 (including packet structure)
- IPv4 address exhaustion
- IPv6 (and packet structure)
- List of IP protocol numbers
- Packet
- TCP and UDP port numbers
- TDM
- Transmission Control Protocol

References

[1] Netgear ProSafe XSM7224S reference manual

[2] Siyan, Karanjit. *Inside TCP/IP*, New Riders Publishing, 1997. ISBN 1-56205-714-6

[3] Basic Journey of a Packet (http://www.securityfocus.com/infocus/1870)

[4] Vinton G. Cerf, Robert E. Kahn, "A Protocol for Packet Network Intercommunication", IEEE Transactions on Communications, Vol. 22, No. 5, May 1974 pp. 637-648

[5] CIO council adds to IPv6 transition primer (http://www.gcn.com/print/25_16/41051-1.html), gcn.com

[6] Theregister.com (http://www.theregister.co.uk/2004/07/06/ipv9_hype_dismissed/)

[7] RFC 1606: *A Historical Perspective On The Usage Of IP Version 9*. April 1, 1994.

[8] Security Assessment of the Internet Protocol (IP)(archived version) (http://web.archive.org/web/20100211145721/http://www.cpni. gov.uk/Docs/InternetProtocol.pdf)

[9] Security Assessment of the Internet Protocol version 4 (IPv4) (http://tools.ietf.org/html/draft-ietf-opsec-ip-security)

External links

- Internet Protocol (http://www.dmoz.org/Computers/Internet/Protocols/) at the Open Directory Project
- RFC 791
- Data Communication Lectures of Manfred Lindner - Part IP Technology Basics (http://www.ict.tuwien.ac.at/ lva/384.081/infobase/L30-IP_Technology_Basics_v4-6.pdf)
- Data Communication Lectures of Manfred Lindner - Part IP Technology Details (http://www.ict.tuwien.ac.at/ lva/384.081/infobase/L31-IP_Technology_Details_v4-7.pdf)
- Data Communication Lectures of Manfred Lindner - Part IPv6 (http://www.ict.tuwien.ac.at/lva/384.081/ infobase/L80-IPv6_v4-6.pdf)
- IPv6.com - Knowledge Center for Next Generation Internet IPv6 (http://www.ipv6.com)

General_Packet_Radio_Service

General packet radio service (GPRS) is a packet oriented mobile data service on the 2G and 3G cellular communication system's global system for mobile communications (GSM). GPRS was originally standardized by European Telecommunications Standards Institute (ETSI) in response to the earlier CDPD and i-mode packet-switched cellular technologies. It is now maintained by the 3rd Generation Partnership Project (3GPP).[1] [2]

GPRS usage is typically charged based on volume of data. This contrasts with circuit switching data, which is typically billed per minute of connection time, regardless of whether or not the user transfers data during that period.

GPRS data is typically supplied either as part of a bundle (e.g., 5 GB per month for a fixed fee) or on a pay-as-you-use basis. Usage above the bundle cap is either charged per megabyte or disallowed. The pay-as-you-use charging is typically per megabyte of traffic.

GPRS is a best-effort service, implying variable throughput and latency that depend on the number of other users sharing the service concurrently, as opposed to circuit switching, where a certain quality of service (QoS) is guaranteed during the connection. In 2G systems, GPRS provides data rates of 56–114 kbit/second.[3] 2G cellular technology combined with GPRS is sometimes described as *2.5G*, that is, a technology between the second (2G) and third (3G) generations of mobile telephony.[4] It provides moderate-speed data transfer, by using unused time division multiple access (TDMA) channels in, for example, the GSM system. GPRS is integrated into GSM Release 97 and newer releases.

Technical overview

The GPRS core network allows 2G, 3G and WCDMA mobile networks to transmit IP packets to external networks such as the Internet. The GPRS system is an integrated part of the GSM network switching subsystem.

Services offered

GPRS extends the GSM Packet circuit switched data capabilities and makes the following services possible:

- SMS messaging and broadcasting
- "Always on" internet access
- Multimedia messaging service (MMS)
- Push to talk over cellular (PoC)
- Instant messaging and presence—wireless village
- Internet applications for smart devices through wireless application protocol (WAP)
- Point-to-point (P2P) service: inter-networking with the Internet (IP)
- Point-to-Multipoint (P2M) service: point-to-multipoint multicast and point-to-multipoint group calls

If SMS over GPRS is used, an SMS transmission speed of about 30 SMS messages per minute may be achieved. This is much faster than using the ordinary SMS over GSM, whose SMS transmission speed is about 6 to 10 SMS messages per minute.

Protocols supported

GPRS supports the following protocols:

- Internet protocol IP. In practice, built-in mobile browsers use IPv4 since IPv6 was not yet popular.
- Point-to-point protocol (PPP). In this mode PPP is often not supported by the mobile phone operator but if the mobile is used as a modem to the connected computer, PPP is used to tunnel IP to the phone. This allows an IP address to be assigned dynamically to the mobile equipment.
- X.25 connections. This is typically used for applications like wireless payment terminals, although it has been removed from the standard. X.25 can still be supported over PPP, or even over IP, but doing this requires either a network based router to perform encapsulation or intelligence built in to the end-device/terminal; e.g., user equipment (UE).

When TCP/IP is used, each phone can have one or more IP addresses allocated. GPRS will store and forward the IP packets to the phone even during handover. The TCP handles any packet loss (e.g. due to a radio noise induced pause).

Hardware

Devices supporting GPRS are divided into three classes:

Class A

> Can be connected to GPRS service and GSM service (voice, SMS), using both at the same time. Such devices are known to be available today.

Class B

> Can be connected to GPRS service and GSM service (voice, SMS), but using only one or the other at a given time. During GSM service (voice call or SMS), GPRS service is suspended, and then resumed automatically after the GSM service (voice call or SMS) has concluded. Most GPRS mobile devices are Class B.

Class C

> Are connected to either GPRS service or GSM service (voice, SMS). Must be switched manually between one or the other service.

A true Class A device may be required to transmit on two different frequencies at the same time, and thus will need two radios. To get around this expensive requirement, a GPRS mobile may implement the dual transfer mode (DTM) feature. A DTM-capable mobile may use simultaneous voice and packet data, with the network coordinating to ensure that it is not required to transmit on two different frequencies at the same time. Such mobiles are considered pseudo-Class A, sometimes referred to as "simple class A". Some networks support DTM since 2007.

USB 3G/GPRS modems use a terminal-like interface over USB 1.1, 2.0 and later, data formats V.42bis, and RFC 1144 and some models have connector for external antenna. Modems can be added as cards (for laptops) or external USB devices which are similar in shape and size to a computer mouse, or nowadays more like a pendrive.

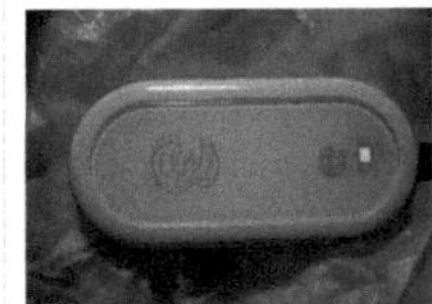

Huawei E220 3G/GPRS Modem

Addressing

A GPRS connection is established by reference to its access point name (APN). The APN defines the services such as wireless application protocol (WAP) access, short message service (SMS), multimedia messaging service (MMS), and for Internet communication services such as email and World Wide Web access.

In order to set up a GPRS connection for a wireless modem, a user must specify an APN, optionally a user name and password, and very rarely an IP address, all provided by the network operator.

Coding schemes and speeds

The upload and download speeds that can be achieved in GPRS depend on a number of factors such as:

- the number of BTS TDMA time slots assigned by the operator
- the channel encoding is used.
- the maximum capability of the mobile device expressed as a GPRS multislot class

Multiple access schemes

The multiple access methods used in GSM with GPRS are based on frequency division duplex (FDD) and TDMA. During a session, a user is assigned to one pair of up-link and down-link frequency channels. This is combined with time domain statistical multiplexing; i.e., packet mode communication, which makes it possible for several users to share the same frequency channel. The packets have constant length, corresponding to a GSM time slot. The down-link uses first-come first-served packet scheduling, while the up-link uses a scheme very similar to reservation ALOHA (R-ALOHA). This means that slotted ALOHA (S-ALOHA) is used for reservation inquiries during a contention phase, and then the actual data is transferred using dynamic TDMA with first-come first-served scheduling.

Channel encoding

Channel encoding is based on a convolutional code at different code rates and GMSK modulation defined for GSM. The following table summarises the options:

Coding scheme	Speed (kbit/s)
CS-1	8.0
CS-2	12.0
CS-3	14.4
CS-4	20.0

The least robust, but fastest, coding scheme (CS-4) is available near a base transceiver station (BTS), while the most robust coding scheme (CS-1) is used when the mobile station (MS) is further away from a BTS.

Using the CS-4 it is possible to achieve a user speed of 20.0 kbit/s per time slot. However, using this scheme the cell coverage is 25% of normal. CS-1 can achieve a user speed of only 8.0 kbit/s per time slot, but has 98% of normal coverage. Newer network equipment can adapt the transfer speed automatically depending on the mobile location.

In addition to GPRS, there are two other GSM technologies which deliver data services: circuit-switched data (CSD) and high-speed circuit-switched data (HSCSD). In contrast to the shared nature of GPRS, these instead establish a dedicated circuit (usually billed per minute). Some applications such as video calling may prefer HSCSD, especially when there is a continuous flow of data between the endpoints.

The following table summarises some possible configurations of GPRS and circuit switched data services.

Technology	Download (kbit/s)	Upload (kbit/s)	TDMA Timeslots allocated (DL+UL)
CSD	9.6	9.6	1+1
HSCSD	28.8	14.4	2+1
HSCSD	43.2	14.4	3+1
GPRS	80.0	20.0 (Class 8 & 10 and CS-4)	4+1
GPRS	60.0	40.0 (Class 10 and CS-4)	3+2
EGPRS (EDGE)	236.8	59.2 (Class 8, 10 and MCS-9)	4+1
EGPRS (EDGE)	177.6	118.4 (Class 10 and MCS-9)	3+2

Multislot Class

The multislot class determines the speed of data transfer available in the Uplink and Downlink directions. It is a value between 1 to 45 which the network uses to allocate radio channels in the uplink and downlink direction. Multislot class with values greater than 31 are referred to as high multislot classes.

A multislot allocation is represented as, for example, 5+2. The first number is the number of downlink timeslots and the second is the number of uplink timeslots allocated for use by the mobile station. A commonly used value is class 10 for many GPRS/EGPRS mobiles which uses a maximum of 4 timeslots in downlink direction and 2 timeslots in uplink direction. However simultaneously a maximum number of 5 simultaneous timeslots can be used in both uplink and downlink. The network will automatically configure the for either 3+2 or 4+1 operation depending on the nature of data transfer.

Some high end mobiles, usually also supporting UMTS also support GPRS/EDGE multislot class 32. According to 3GPP TS 45.002 (Release 6), Table B.2, mobile stations of this class support 5 timeslots in downlink and 3 timeslots in uplink with a maximum number of 6 simultaneously used timeslots. If data traffic is concentrated in downlink direction the network will configure the connection for 5+1 operation. When more data is transferred in the uplink the network can at any time change the constellation to 4+2 or 3+3. Under the best reception conditions, i.e. when the best EDGE modulation and coding scheme can be used, 5 timeslots can carry a bandwidth of 5*59.2 kbit/s = 296 kbit/s. In uplink direction, 3 timeslots can carry a bandwidth of 3*59.2 kbit/s = 177.6 kbit/s.[5]

Multislot Classes for GPRS/EGPRS

Multislot Class	Downlink TS	Uplink TS	Active TS
1	1	1	2
2	2	1	3
3	2	2	3
4	3	1	4
5	2	2	4
6	3	2	4
7	3	3	4
8	4	1	5
9	3	2	5
10	4	2	5
11	4	3	5
12	4	4	5
30	5	1	6
31	5	2	6
32	5	3	6
33	5	4	6
34	5	5	6

Attributes of a multislot class

Each multislot class identifies the following:

- the maximum number of Timeslots that can be allocated on uplink
- the maximum number of Timeslots that can be allocated on downlink
- the total number of timeslots which can be allocated by the network to the mobile
- the time needed for the MS to perform adjacent cell signal level measurement and get ready to transmit
- the time needed for the MS to get ready to transmit
- the time needed for the MS to perform adjacent cell signal level measurement and get ready to receive
- the time needed for the MS to get ready to receive.

The different multislot class specification is detailed in the Annex B of the 3GPP Technical Specification 45.002 (Multiplexing and multiple access on the radio path)

Usability

The maximum speed of a GPRS connection offered in 2003 was similar to a modem connection in an analog wire telephone network, about 32–40 kbit/s, depending on the phone used. Latency is very high; round-trip time (RTT) is typically about 600–700 ms and often reaches 1 s. GPRS is typically prioritized lower than speech, and thus the quality of connection varies greatly.

Devices with latency/RTT improvements (via, for example, the extended UL TBF mode feature) are generally available. Also, network upgrades of features are available with certain operators. With these enhancements the active round-trip time can be reduced, resulting in significant increase in application-level throughput speeds.

See also

- Code division multiple access (CDMA)
- Enhanced data rates for GSM evolution (EDGE)
- Universal mobile telephone system (UMTS)
- GPRS core network
- Sub-network dependent convergence protocol (SNDCP)
- IP Multimedia Subsystem
- High-speed downlink packet access (HSDPA)
- Cellular data communication protocol
- List of device bandwidths

References

[1] ETSI (http://www.etsi.org/WebSite/homepage.aspx)

[2] http://www.3gpp.org/3GPP

[3] General packet radio service from Qkport (http://about.qkport.com/g/general_packet_radio_service)

[4] Mobile Phone Generations from (http://www.funsms.net/mobile_phone_generations.htm)

[5] http://mobilesociety.typepad.com/mobile_life/2007/04/gprs_and_edge_m.html

External links

- 3GPP AT command set for user equipment (UE) (http://www.3gpp.org/ftp/Specs/latest/Rel-8/27_series/27007-841.zip)
- GPRS security information (archive.org) (http://web.archive.org/web/20080209213430/http://www.gprssecurity.com/)
- Free GPRS resources (http://www.telecomspace.com/datatech-gprs.html)
- Free online tutorial (http://www.comsoc.org/livepubs/surveys/public/3q99issue/bettstetter.html).
- GSM World, the trade association for GSM and GPRS network operators (http://www.gsmworld.com/technology/gprs/intro.shtml).
- Palowireless GPRS resource center (http://www.palowireless.com/gprs/)
- GPRS attach and PDP context activation sequence diagram (http://www.eventhelix.com/RealtimeMantra/Telecom/gprs_attach_pdp_sequence_diagram.pdf)

Article Sources and Contributors

Network_forensics *Source*: http://en.wikipedia.org/w/index.php?title=Network_forensics *Contributors*: Bearcat, Cwmhiraeth, David Eppstein, Emmshub, ErrantX, Kvng, Nz26, Ospalh, Ray3055, Schoetti, TimBentley, Wafoijoi99, Woohookitty, 10 anonymous edits

Digital_forensics *Source*: http://en.wikipedia.org/w/index.php?title=Digital_forensics *Contributors*: Antrim Kate, Autoerrant, Cadava14, Chowbok, Christian75, Daskalak, ErrantX, Jappalang, Jim Sweeney, John of Reading, Jrtayloriv, Ling.Nut, Malleus Fatuorum, ProloSozz, Raeky, SuperMarioMan, Tabletop, The Anome, ToddWC, TonyTheTiger, Will Beback Auto, Wlodzimierz, Zundark, 10 anonymous edits

Computer_network *Source*: http://en.wikipedia.org/w/index.php?title=Computer_network *Contributors*: *Kat*, 10metreh, 149AFK, 16@r, 1966batfan, 28421u2232nfenfcenc, 28bytes, 2D, 5 albert square, 802geek, A520, ACBest, AJCham, ARUNKUMAR P.R, Aajaja, Abb615, Abraham, B.S., Acnetj, Adam1213, Adam850, Adambro, Addihockey10, AdjustShift, AeonicOmega, Aeonx, Aicchalmers, Aij, Aitias, Ajl772, Akb.pcb, Akendall, Alansohn, Aleenf1, AlexiusHoratius, Allens, Alpha 4615, Alphachimp, Altruism, Alucard 16, Amirrad.en, Andrew D White, Andrewcrawford, Andy16666, Aneah, Angrysockhop, Anna Lincoln, Anonauthor, Anonymi, Antandrus, Anupkeskar, Apau98, Apparition11, Apteva, Arctic Fox, ArglebargleIV, Armchair info guy, ArmenSokhakyan, Arthena, Atw1996, Avinash0147, Avoided, Avril0412, AzaToth, Banaticus, Baronnet, Bart133, Bassbonerocks, Beelaj, Bella Swan, Belovedfreak, BevinBrett, Bhasrini, Bjankuloski06en, Black Falcon, Blanchardb, Blaxthos, Blazerskj7315, BlueDevil, Bluerasberry, Bob f it, Bobby122, Bobo192, Bogey97, Bokunenjin, Bongwarrior, Brandon, Brian Crawford, Btilm, BuddhaBubba, Bumpusjames, Bushsf, ButOnMethItIs, Bwmitche, Bxn1358, C777, CBM, CWY2190, CWii, Cachiadavid, Caiaffa, Calltech, Caltas, Camw, Can You Prove That You're Human, Can't sleep, clown will eat me, CanadianLinuxUser, CapitalR, Capricorn42, Captain panda, Captain-tucker, Captainreiss, CardinalDan, Cbdorsett, Cerebellum, CesarB, Cgmusselman, Chad44, Chakkalokesh, Chandlermbing, Chris the speller, Chrisch, Chriswiki, Chromaticity, Chzz, Clarince63, Closedmouth, Cnilep, Cnkids, Coeus559, CommonsDelinker, Corruptcopper, Courcelles, Cpiral, Cpl Syx, Cst17, Cstratacos, Cwilso, Cwoodskareska, Cxz111, Cybercobra, Cyclonenim, D, D. Recorder, D.c.camero, DARTH SIDIOUS 2, DJBullfish, Dabomb87, Dac04, DakotaDAllen, DaltinWentsworth, DanMS, Daniel Procter, Danlaycock, Dap263, Darkkloud29, Darth Panda, Davosmith, Dayyanb, DeadEyeArrow, Decltype, Demonslayer4000, Denisarona, DerHexer, Dgtsyb, Dgw, Diannaa, Dicklyon, Dipankan001, Discospinster, Djg2006, Djmckee1, Dlohcierekim, Dotancohen, DoubleBlue, Download, Dreadstar, Dwayne, DyingIce, Dylan620, EarthPerson, Easwarno1, Eeekster, Eggnogicecream, Egmontaz, Eitheladar, Eleos, Elinruby, Elphion, Emailtonaved, EncMstr, Enigmaman, Epbr123, Er Komandante, Eraxx, Erdoğan said, Erianna, Eric-Wester, Escape Orbit, EvokeNZ, Excirial, Extransit, FJPB, Face, Faithlessthewonderboy, Falcon8765, Faradayplank, Favonian, FayssalF, Fazlurrahman95, Fgrose, Fieldday-sunday, Fiftwekid, Figma, Finnysgay, Fintanmurphy, Fireaxe888, Fireice, Firien, Flewis, Flyingcheese, Fozz79, Frankie0607, Freedomlinux, Frmatt, Funnyfarmofdoom, Fyyer, Fæ, GLaDOS, GNMC, Gail, GandalfDaGraay, Gholam, Giftlite, Glane23, Glenn, Gnowor, Gogo Dodo, GoingBatty, Gonchibolso12, GoneAwayNowAndRetired, Grafen, Greenrd, GroveGuy, Guggfe, Gurch, Gurchzilla, Gyan pokhara, Hammersoft, Happysailor, HarisM, Harryzilber, Harshrateria, Haseo9999, Hcberkowitz, Hchrm, Headbomb, Hellokittylover12, Hemachandra18, Herbythyme, HiDrNick, Hpcanswers, Hut 8.5, INkubusse, Ianmillner, Igoldste, Imroy, Incompetence, Indon, Inseeisyou, Intgr, Ipatrol, Iridescent, IronGargoyle, It4it-wiki, Itusg15q4user, J. Martin Wills, J.delanoy, JBazuzi, JEBrown87544, JLRedperson, JLaTondre, Jackelfive, Jackfork, Jackol, Jake Wartenberg, Jan1nad, Japheth the Warlock, Jared Preston, Jasper Deng, Jauerback, Jay, Jayakrishnan0804, Jclemens, Jeepday, Jeff G., Jer71, Jerzy, Jflabourdette, Jheyahr, Jimmi Hugh, Jjasi, Jjensen347, Jjron, Jni, Joantorres, Joelhanley, John Stumbles, Johnuniq, JonHarder, Jordanfeldman, Joseph Solis in Australia, Joshua Gyamfi, Joshua Scott, Joy, Jpbowen, Jxl180, KGasso, Kazochi, Kbrose, Keilana, KelleyCook, Kgfleischmann, Kieferb12, King of Hearts, Kingpin13, Kms, KnowBuddy, Knowz, Koffieyahoo, Koolabsol, Kozuch, Kranix, Krishnavedala, Krj373, Kudret abi, Kvng, L Kensington, L314t, L33th4x0rguy, LFaraone, Landon1980, Leafyplant, LeaveSleaves, LeinaD natipaC, Levineps, Leye1, Lightmouse, Lights, LilHelpa, Lilac Soul, Lillightning, Limideen, LindsayH, Ling.Nut, Loile0801, Lotje, Lucky arien2001, Ludovic.ferre, Luk, Lukeritchie, MER-C, Macbookmiller, Macy, Madcoverboy, Madhero88, Magioladitis, Maismuhanad, Mandarax, Maneendra, Manjax76, Marco94, Marek69, Mark Arsten, Mark91, MarkBolton, Markdude09, MarkmacVSS, Mascharanas, Masterjamie, Matdrodes, Mattgirling, Mattl2001, McSly, Mdd, Mentifisto, Mephistophelian, Metricopolus, Michael Angelkovich, Michael93555, Micke-sv, Mikaey, Mike Rosoft, Mike.lifeguard, MikhailVS, Milind m2255, Mindmatrix, Minimac, Minimac's Clone, Misortie, MisterCharlie, Miym, Mlewis000, Mlouns, Mmernex, Mmmeg, Modamoda, Montchav, Montrevux, MorrisRob, Mottsauce, Mr. Wheely Guy, MrSmook, Mrnatural, MuZemike, Muhandes, My76Strat, Mynameiswill, N5iln, Nanzilla, Nathanid, NawlinWiki, Nazi 2007, Neillucas, NeoJustin, Nepenthes, Netalarm, Nethgirb, Netito777, Networkingguy, NewEnglandYankee, Ngriffeth, Nihiltres, Nopetro, Northamerica1000, NorwegianBlue, NoticeBored, Novalis, Nrm123, Nsda, Nubiatech, Nurg, Nurlan926, Ojasweesharma, Oliver202, OllieFury, Onure, Opelio, Orange Suede Sofa, Orbst, Oroso, Otolemur crassicaudatus, OverlordQ, Oxymoron83, PAntoni, Padillah, Pakakj.20june, Pascal.Tesson, PatrikR, Paul August, Pchov, Pdcook, Pedro, Peterwhy, PhJ, Pharaoh of the Wizards, Phatom87, PhilKnight, Philip Trueman, PhilipJS, Phoe6, Piano non troppo, Pigman, Pill, Pinethicket, Pingveno, Plaga701, PleaseStand, Polluxian, Porkrind, Porterjoh, Possum, Poweroid, Prari, Prashanthns, Promethean, Public Menace, Puffin, Pwarrior, Pxma, Pyrospirit, Quaeler, Quantpole, Qwyrxian, Qxz, R'n'B, RJaguar3, RadioFan, Radon210, Raed abu farha, Rahul440, RainbowOfLight, Rananera74, Rangek, Rangoon11, Raven21421, Razarajpoot, Razertek, Rctay, Reaper Eternal, Red Thrush, Reliableforever, Rememberway, Renewer, Rettetast, Riana, Ricardoprojects, Rick Block, Riick, Rmaheshnaidu, Rmosler2100, RoMo37, RobertIllston, Roland Kaufmann, Rpsjrcpa, Rsrikanth05, Rwwww, RyanCross, Ryulong, SMC, ST47, Saketmitra, Sandeepsp4u, Satori Son, Sayedomer, Scgtrp, Sciurinæ, Scottywong, Seaphoto, Seek54, Sephiroth BCR, Sesu Prime, Sgeo, Shadowjams, Shanes, Shenme, Shiwakant.bharti, ShornAssociates, Sigma 7, Skarebo, Skizzik, SkyWalker, Skyezx, Slawekb, Slon02, SmartGuy Old, Smokizzy, SoCalSuperEagle, Soap Poisoning, Some jerk on the Internet, Sonjaaa, SpaceFlight89, SpecMode, Special Cases, Spitfire, Spmeyn, SpuriousQ, Srikarkashyap, Ssmorris, StaleOnion, SteinbDJ, Stephan Leeds, Stephenb, SteveO, Storm Rider, Stwalkerster, SudoGhost, Suffusion of Yellow, Sumitprksh, SuperSlacker, Symetrix, Synchronism, Syrthiss, Tango, Tarif Ezaz, Tbhotch, Teapeat, TechTWI, Technobadger, Terrek, Testbells, Tgeairn, The Thing That Should Not Be, TheCatalyst31, Thedjatclubrock, Thejokerface, Thetaung, Think outside the box, Thrindel, Thumperward, Tiddly Tom, Tide rolls, Titoxd, Todd Peng, Tombomp, Tony1, Topbanana, Toussaint, Traxs7, Trenwith, TreveX, Trgaz, Triona, Triwbe, Tropryor, Tslocum, Turabsf, Turgan, TutterMouse, TyA, Tyrol5, UBJ 43X, UU, Ultimarko, Uncle Dick, UncleDouggie, Vamphemu, VandalCruncher, Vanished user 39948282, Vanka5, Versageek, Versus22, VictorAnyakin, Visaforu, Visor, VooDooChild, Vrenator, W Nowicki, Wa3frp, Wadamja, Walter.bender, Waryklingon, Watchdog9, Wbm1058, Weezey, Welsh, Whereizben, WhisperToMe, WikHead, Wikipelli, Wikipixel, Wilde Jagd, Wimt, Wine Guy, Winston Chuen-Shih Yang, Wizardist, Wknight94, Wolfkeeper, Woohookitty, Wtmitchell, Wtsao, Wuhwuzdat, Xompanthy, YassineMrabet, Zawthet, Zedex7, Zentraleinheite, Zzuuzz, בּוּבּبحم, شاش تاتوصيّ, 05 وجرتم أكانرت, סה، סה־סה, 2806 anonymous edits

Intrusion_detection_system *Source*: http://en.wikipedia.org/w/index.php?title=Intrusion_detection_system *Contributors*: (, Aapo Laitinen, Aaryna, Abune, Access-bb, Aghsajjy, Alima86, Andrew.philip.thomas, Aneah, Anubis1055, Astronautics, Baszerr, Bender235, Bernolákovčina, BigChicken, Bluefoxicy, Bomazi, Bond0088, Boonebytes, Borgx, Boundary11, Btornado, Butseriouslyfolks, Caffeinepuppy, Capricorn42, Charlesrh, Chowbok, Clangin, CliffC, CraigMonroe, CrazyChemGuy, DMacks, Dcampbell130, Ddasune, Denoir, Derekrogerson, Difference engine, Discospinster, Dremeda, Drphilharmonic, EdC, Ellywa, Falcon Kirtaran, Falcon9x5, Ferengi, Finity, FleetCommand, Footballfan190, Fossguy, Frap, GattoRandagio, Gtrmp, Gunnar Kreitz, Guy Harris, H2g2bob, Haiauphixu, Harperf, Hashar, Hellisp, Hiihammuk, Hotmixclass, Intgr, Isnow, J7387438, Jasonhatwiki, Jclemens, Jerryobject, Jesse5656, Jim1138, JonHarder, Joonga, Josh3580, Jovianeye, Joy, JurgenHadley, Karthikjain, Kernel.package, Kolmigabrouil, Kpcatch6, Kravietz, Krille, Kuru, Lady Tenar, Lamf 0009, Lokipro, M3tainfo, Madhero88, MarkSutton, Mav, Michael Hardy, Michael@thelander.com, Midnightcomm, Mintleaf, Mmernex, MrOllie, Msoos, Najoj, NeilN, NewEnglandYankee, Ngardiner, Nhero2006, Nitin.skd, Nuno Tavares, Oakleeman, Obradovic Goran, Olivier Debre, Omarmalali, Paklan, PhilKnight, Phisches, PhnomPencil, PolarYukon, Qrsdogg, Qxz, RA0808, RISCO Group, Radagast83, Rick Block, Rick Sidwell, Rjwilmsi, Ronhjones, Ronz, Schneelocke, Sgorton, Shadowjams, Shahmirj, Sietse Snel, Simmondp, Sir Vicious, Slakr, Smaffy, Some jerk on the Internet, Studerby, Sysy, Tackat, Tamer ih, Tburket, Thecheesykid, Tje, Tmh, Tobias Bergemann, UU, Unforgettableid, Visnup, Weregerbil, Wereon, Willsmith, Wilson.canadian, Windharp, Wolfmankurd, Yms, 334 anonymous edits

Digital_evidence *Source*: http://en.wikipedia.org/w/index.php?title=Digital_evidence *Contributors*: BD2412, ClementSeveillac, DanielCD, DerHexer, Deville, Doldrums, Dpv, Eastlaw, ErrantX, Glines, Iangfc, JLaTondre, Mmmbeer, Modify, Muhandes, PeetMoss, Praveen Dalal, Ralphlosey, Rjwilmsi, Rwwww, SCEhardt, Sardanaphalus, 22 anonymous edits

Computer_forensics *Source*: http://en.wikipedia.org/w/index.php?title=Computer_forensics *Contributors*: AC, ALargeElk, Aa999uk, Abune, Action grrl, Afcyrus, Ajcblyth, AlMac, Aladdin Sane, Alexandru47, Algae, Alistair.phillips1, Altordwm, Aluion, Amars, Andreworkney, Aneah, Apoc2400, Appraiser, Arichnad, ArnoldReinhold, Asyndeton, Avraham, B-Con, Bbouquet, Bchertoff, Bender235, Binarygal, BirgitteSB, Bloodshedder, BlueAmethyst, Bmgoldbe, Bobrayner, Borgx, Brandonjelinek, Bulldawg9908, CB79, Cadava14, Callidior, CanisRufus, Cappleby-dborkowski, Centrx, Ceyockey, Charlene.fic, Chillum, Chris the speller, Chris83, ChrisGualtieri, ChrisWagoner, Christina Silverman, Cinnamon42, Cloizides mmacnicol, Comte0, Cralar, Cupids wings, DGX, Dancontiki, DanielCD, DanielPharos, Dark AQ, Daskalak, Dave Cohoe, Dcirovic, Dcoetzee, Dekisugi, Dhendron, Diana.todi, Dianeburley, Digicurator, DigitalMediaInvestigators, Digitalx86, Disklabs, DocWatson42, Dontaskme, Dreadstar, Drpickem, Dspradau, Długosz, EagleFan, Editus Reloaded, El C, Enarche, Epitome83, Ericjhuber, ErrantX, Felipe1982, Finalius, Forensicsguru, Frank Kai Fat Chow, Frap, Freber1977, G Clark, GCarty, Gajedi, Gdardick, Gene.arboit, Ghaly, Glane23, Glorymanu, Gogo Dodo, GraemeL, Grolltech, GroupOne, H.sanat, HJ Mitchell, Har-Magedon, Hazard-SJ, Honeyjew, Hu12, ISFCE, Iamsquare, Igoldste, Intgr, J.delanoy, Jafeluv, Janguilano, Janke, Jasperloco, JayC, Jbeacontec, Jerzy, Jessekornblum, Jgfoot, Jimregan, JonHarder, Jonathankrause, Jonnychu, Joy, Justinc, Jwbang, Karrde73, Kbdank71, KesslerInternational, Kesslerintl, Khanssen, Khoikhoi, Krashlandon, Krellis, Kuru, Kushwadhwa, L33tb0b, Ligulem, LinuxAngel, MSR, MacStep, Mahanga, Mboverload, Merovingian, Midnightcomm, Mike.lifeguard, Mike6271, Mindmatrix, Mmernex, Mmmbeer, Modify, Monty845, Moreschi, MrOllie, Mrld, Mrmiscellanious, Mygerardromance, Nabokov, Nageh, Natural Born Devastator, Necrothesp, Newsmare, Nivix, Nuwewsco, Orbframe, Orison316, Pacifistpanda, Pascal666, PeterFisk, Peterb323, Phagen6368, PinchasC, Pinephilips, Pmboogie, Pndfam05, Pneidig, Praveen Dalal, Pseudo clever, Public Menace, Radagast83, Random name, Randy Johnston, Rasriis, Rattatosk, Reedy, ResidueOfDesign, Rjwilmsi, Rklawton, Rl244, Rmislan, Robert Bond, Robklpd, Rodolico, Ron Barker, Roux-HG, Rurik, Sanguinity, Santoshrautforensic, SchfiftyThree, Schoetti, Semanresu, Shoombooly, Shumdw, Simsong, Smoshlak, Speisert, Splintercellguy, Srhinesmith, Suryatejag, TOMA4ATO MONSTAH, Tbhotch, Tero, Texture, Th1rt3en, The Anome, TheWeasel, Themfromspace, Thiseye, Thorbjørn Ellefsen, Tide rolls, TimBentley, TimVickers, Tizio, Toddst1, TrudySinclaire, Vardanbalyan, Variables, Vicpirate, Vmanoussos, Wafoijoi99, Waggers, Wavelength, Webmaster961, Webucation, Wimt, Withouttrace, Wmahan, Woogee, Ww, Xeon06, Xx0033, Zorry, Zzuuzz, 599 anonymous edits

Ethernet *Source*: http://en.wikipedia.org/w/index.php?title=Ethernet *Contributors*: 0612, 121a0012, 1lovegal, 1stJahman, 4a6f656c, 7, ARC Gritt, Aapo Laitinen, Abdull, Adashiel, AdjustShift, Adrian.benko, Aeluwas, Ahoerstemeier, Ajraddatz, Akriasas, Alan Liefting, Alansohn, Aldie, Ale jrb, Alecv, Algocu, AlistairMcMillan, Altermike, Alvestrand, Alyssapvr, Amatulic, Ameliorate!,

Amillar, Amore proprio, Anaraug, Andareed, Andreas Toth, Andy Dingley, Andybryant, Andyhodapp, Aneah, Angela, Angusmca, Anss123, Applemacintosh10, Arch dude, Arkrishna, Armando, ArnoldReinhold, Artaxiad, AtomEdge, Avono, Azaghal of Belegost, B4hand, BD2412, Bbachrac, Bctwriter, Bdmcmahon, Becritical, Betacommand, Betbest1, BiT, Bidabadi, Bigboymcgee, Bigjimr, Bilbo1507, Biot, BlueAg09, Blutrot, Bobblewik, Boffy b, Bomac, Bookbrad, Bookofjude, Bootleggingly mcbootleg, Boscobiscotti, Bovineone, Branclem, Branko, Brian Patrie, Btilm, Bumm13, Buy P%E%P%S%I, COnanPayne, CRGreathouse, CS46, Calltech, Caltas, CamTarn, Can't sleep, clown will eat me, Capricorn42, Carlo.Ierna, Casey Abell, Catgut, Causantin, Cburnett, CesarB, Chaosgate, Charles Gaudette, Chasingsol, Chealer, Chmod007, Chowbok, Cjdaniel, ClementSeveillac, Closedmouth, CloudNine, Cluth, Cmdrjameson, Colin Marquardt, Conversion script, Corpx, Corti, Corwin8, Cpl Syx, Creidieki, Crispmuncher, Crissov, CryptoDerk, Cstanners, Cybercobra, DVdm, Daa89563, Dachshund, Damian Yerrick, Davehard, David Biddulph, DavidBailey, DavidH, Dcorzine, Deflective, Dennis Brown, Dicklyon, Digitalsushi, Discospinster, Diskdoc, DocWatson42, Dogcow, Donnieleefarrow, Download, Drak2, Drphilharmonic, Dtcdthingy, EEgirl18, EagleOne, Ebear422, Econrad, Eeekster, Efa, Egil, Ehn, Eivind F Øyangen, El Cubano, ElBenevolente, Electron9, Elektrik Shoos, Eleuther, Elinruby, Eloil, Engineerism, Enjoi4586, EoGuy, Epbr123, Evil genius, Ewlyahoocom, Excirial, Facts707, Femto, Fenrisulfr, Fetofs, Fieldday-sunday, Finest1, Firsfron, Flewis, FocalPoint, Frankchn, Frap, Fratrep, Fred Bradstadt, Fredrik, Fresheneesz, Fudoreaper, Fulldecent, Furrykef, G4wsz, GTAKIllerEric, Gah4, Gascreed, Geek2003, Gekkoblaster, Generica, Ghaly, Giftlite, Glacialfox, Glenn, Gnalk, Gnuish, Gogo Dodo, Golgofrinchian, Gopher23, Goplat, Gosub, Graham87, Grandsonofmaaden, Greylion, Grgan, Guanxi, Guy Harris, Gyanlakhwani, H0serdude, HCelik, Haakon, Hadal, HappyCamper, Harryzilber, Harvester, Helix84, Herberthuber, Heron, Hobophobe, Hughey, Hungrymouse, Hussein 95, Hvn0413, Iambk, Iamzemasterraf, Ibc111, Idkyididthis, Igoldste, Indefatigable, Intgr, Iridescent, Irq, Isaac Rabinovitch, Itai, Itusg15q4user, J.delanoy, J04n, Jakohn, JamesBWatson, JamesEG, JeLuF, Jec, Jemichel, Jhartmann, Jim.henderson, John a s, JohnOwens, JohnWittle, Johnblade, Johnnyboyshoots, Johnuniq, JonHarder, Joseph507357, Joyous!, Jtkiefer, Juansempere, Judzillah, Juliancolton, K45671, KGasso, Kakomu, KaragouniS, Karn, Kate.woodcroft, Kbh3rd, Kbolino, Kbrose, Keith D, KelleyCook, Kerotan, Kevmcs, Kgfleischmann, Khalad, Kinema, King of Hearts, Kjkolb, Knucmo2, Kuru, Kvng, Kwamikagami, Kwiki, Lamro, Laudaka, Lavenderbunny, Lee Carre, Leebo, Leotohill, Lightmouse, Ligulem, LilHelpa, Limbo socrates, LittleBenW, LittleOldMe, Lockg, Lolpack, LordJumper, Lotu, Lovecz, Lped999, Lukith, Lumos3, Luna Santin, MER-C, MacGyverMagic, Mahjongg, Makeemlighter, Manish soni, Markjx, Martarius, Martijn Hoekstra, Matt.farina, Maury Markowitz, Mav, Mbutts, Melvinvon, Mendel, MessiFCB, Mhare, Michael Hardy, Michael Slone, Michael Thomas Sullivan, MightyWarrior, Mightyms, Mike Rosoft, Mikm, Milan Keršláger, Mindmatrix, Minesweeper, Mmiszka, Modulatum, Mortense, MoussePad, Moxfyre, Mozzerati, MrFish, MrOllie, Mrand, Mrh30, Mwanner, Myanw, N TRoPY, NJM, NawlinWiki, NeaNita, Nelson50, NewEnglandYankee, Nicolaasuni, Nightraider0, Nikevich, Nimiew, Nishkid64, Nixdorf, Nnemo, Norm, Northamerica1000, Now3d, Nroets, Nthep, Nubiatech, Nvj, Nyttend, Oakad, Ohconfucius, Ohnoitsjamie, Oneocean, OverlordQ, OwenX, Oxymoron83, Packetslinger, Palmer1973, Paul, Paul Koning, Peck123, Pekaje, Percy Snoodle, Peruvianllama, Petrb, Peyre, Pgallert, Pgan002, Phil Boswell, Philip Trueman, Piano non troppo, PierreAbbat, Pilatus, PinkMonkeys, Pjbrockmann, Pkirlin, Plasticup, Plugwash, Pluma, Pmsyyz, Praetor alpha, Prolog, Publicly Visible, QmunkE, Quarl, Quintote, RHaworth, RadioFan, Rait, Rapaporta, Rarmy, Recurring dreams, RedWolf, Rednectar.chris, Reedy, Requestion, Rettetast, Rhobite, Rholton, Rich Farmbrough, RichardBennett, Rick Sidwell, Ricsi, Rjwilmsi, Rlcantwell, RoySmith, Roybadami, Royote, Rror, Rsrikanth05, Rufus210, Ruud Koot, Rw4nd4, Rwwww, SF007, SHCarter, Salsa Shark, Sam Hocevar, Sander123, Sceptre, Schneelocke, Scott McNay, ScottJ, SeaChanger, Selmo, Setu, Sfisher, Shadowjams, Shanes, Sharkford, Shieldforyoureyes, Sietse Snel, Silenceisfoo, Sincoskie, Sligocki, SoSaysChappy, Sobelbob, SpamBilly, Spiritia, Steeev, Stephan Leeds, Stephenb, Steven Luo, Stratocracy, Stuart P. Bentley, Suruena, Svick, Swapdisk, Swarnabhra, TAnthony, Tas50, Tedernst, Template namespace initialisation script, Tempodivalse, Thaas00, The Anome, The Random Editor, The Thing That Should Not Be, The quark, The undertow, TheMoog, Thingg, Thue, TimBovee, Tiny plastic Grey Knight, Tizio, Tmontalv, TomPhil, Tonsofpcs, Tooki, Tothwolf, Tpbradbury, Transmission 1000, Trev M, Tunnie, Turgan, Tverbeek, Typo47, Tyz, UU, Ukexpat, Ulric1313, Unschool, Urvabara, Useight, Utuado, Vashti, Vdm, Veinor, Versus22, Vidmes, Vijaykumar, Viridae, Vmenkov, W Nowicki, Wa2ise, WadeSimMiser, Wasisnt, Wattlesmorse, Wavelength, Wayfarer, WaysToEscape, Wbenton, Wbm1058, Wefa, WhiteDragon, Wik, WikiJaZon, Wikiborg, Wikifranz, WillAndrews, WillLord, Willy on Wheels over Ethernet, Wimt, Wingnutamj, Wk muriithi, Wmahan, Wmasterj, Woohookitty, WriterHound, Wrs1864, Wtshymanski, Xenium, Xnatedawgx, Yintan, Yudiweb, Yuvalnod, Yyy, ZenerV, Zero10one, Zhangyue, Zodon, Zoicon5, 995 anonymous edits

Internet_Protocol *Source*: http://en.wikipedia.org/w/index.php?title=Internet_Protocol *Contributors*: 2w133, A-moll9, A. B., ARUNKUMAR P.R, Abb615, Abdull, Adagio Cantabile, Addihockey10, Aekton, Aggelos.Biboudis, Ahoerstemeier, Aldie, Altesys, Alvin-cs, Andareed, Andre Engels, Andywandy, Angelo.biboudis, Anon lynx, Antiuser, Anttin, Anwar saadat, Ardonik, Arkrishna, Attilios, BAxelrod, Badanedwa, Bdesham, Beefman, Bennor, Bentogoa, Biot, Bjornwireen, Blanchardb, Blehfu, Blue520, Bobguy7, Bobo192, Borislav, Brest, Brianga, Bridgecross, Brim, Brouhaha, Bryan Derksen, Bryanbuang1993, CALR, Calltech, Camilo Sanchez, Capricorn42, Caramdir, Carlo.Ierna, Casey Abell, Cbdorsett, Cburnett, Cdyson37, Ceo, CesarB, Chealer, Chenzw, Christian List, Closedmouth, Conversion script, Coolcaesar, Coralmizu, Corruptcopper, Courcelles, Cverska, Cwolfsheep, Cybercobra, Cyclonenim, Cynthia Rhoads, DARTH SIDIOUS 2, Dan D. Ric, Daniel Staal, Daniel.Cardenas, DanielCD, DeadEyeArrow, Defyant, Demian12358, Denisarona, Dgw, Dmaftei, Dnas, Doria, DrBag, Drugonot, Dwheeler, EagleOne, Echuck215, Eclipsed, Eequor, El C, Elfguy, Enjoi4586, Epbr123, Erodium, EverGreg, Evil saltine, FGont, Felipe1982, Ferkelparade, Fish147, Florentino floro, Formulax, Forton, Fredrik, FrummerThanThou, Fæ, Galoubet, Gamera2, GaryW, General Wesc, Giftlite, Glane23, Glenn, Goatbilly, Graciella, GraemeL, Grafen, Graham87, Granbarreman, GreenRoot, Hairy Dude, Hardyplants, Harvester, Hayabusa future, Helix84, Hemanshu, Hetar, Hughcharlesparker, I am Me true, IRedRat, Iamregin, Imcdnzl, Imroy, Intgr, Ixfd64, J.delanoy, JHolman, JTN, Jack Phoenix, Jadounrahul, JamesBWatson, Jasper Deng, Jauhienij, JavierMC, Jdforrester, Jedysurya, Jeff Carr, Jheiv, Jiddisch, Jimgeorge, Jimys salonika, Jnc, Jno, JohnGrantNineTiles, JonHarder, Justsee, KD5TVI, Karl McClendon, Karol Langner, Katalaveno, Kbrose, Kgfleischmann, Kim Bruning, Kocio, Krellis, Kubigula, Kukini, Kvng, L Kensington, Latitudinarian, Liangent, Lion789, Looxix, Lotje, Love manjeet kumar singh, Maerk, Mahabub398, Mailtomeet, Mammad2002, Mange01, Manop, ManuelGR, Markr123, Marr75, Max Naylor, Melter, Mike Rosoft, Mikieminnow, Mindmatrix, Mion, NGNWiki, Naive cynic, Nakon, NawlinWiki, NeoNorm, Nialldawson, Nightraider0, Nimiew, Nixdorf, Noformation, Noldoaran, Northamerica1000, Nubcaike, Nubiatech, Nugzthepirate, O, Ogress, Olathe, Otolemur crassicaudatus, Oxymoron83, Paolopal, Patrick, Paul, PaulHanson, PedroPVZ, Phatom87, Philip Trueman, Pinkadelica, Piotrus, Plustgarten, Poeloq, Poweroid, Ppchailley, Python eggs, Rabbit67890, Recognizance, Reedy, Reub2000, Rgclegg, Rich Farmbrough, Richard Ye, Rjgodoy, Rkrikorian, RobertG, Robocoder, Rsduhamel, Ryamigo, Ryanmcdaniel, Sandstein, SasiSasi, Scientizzle, Scientus, Scopecreep, Senator2029, Shiftoften66, Shlomiz, Shoeofdeath, Sir Arthur Williams, Sjaak, SkyLined, SmilingBoy, Smyth, Some jerk on the Internet, Sonicx059, Sophus Bie, SpaceRocket, SpeedyGonsales, Stephenb, Stevey7788, Supaplex, Suruena, Sysiphe, THEN WHO WAS PHONE?, TakuyaMurata, Tarquin, Teles, Template namespace initialisation script, Tezdog, The Anome, The Transhumanist (AWB), Thorpe, Timwi, Tiuks, TkGy, Tobias Bergemann, Tommy2010, Torla42, Trevor MacInnis, Tristantech, TutterMouse, UncleBubba, Urvabara, V-ball, Varnav, Vary, Versageek, Versus22, VillemVillemVillem, Warren, Wayiran, Wayne Slam, Wcourtney, Wereon, Where, Whitepaw, Wik, Wikibob, Wikisierracharlie, William Avery, Winston Chuen-Shih Yang, Wknight94, Woohookitty, Wrs1864, Wtmitchell, Yahoolian, Yamamoto Ichiro, Yausman, Yidisheryid, Yyy, Zarcillo, Zundark, Zzuuzz, تانيتوص رلاش, කාවිඳ්‍ය, 505 anonymous edits

General_Packet_Radio_Service *Source*: http://en.wikipedia.org/w/index.php?title=General_Packet_Radio_Service *Contributors*: *drew, 24alpha, 4th guy, 63.192.137.xxx, A5b, ALM scientist, Abduljalil859, Abhinavvaid, Abldvlpr, Ahoerstemeier, Alastairgbrown, Ali@gwc.org.uk, AlistairMcMillan, Andrejj, Andros 1337, Andypdavis, Anetode, Angrytoast, Aninhumer, Antonski, Arvinarya, Astronautics, Badanedwa, Baloo rch, Banej, Barneca, Ben-Zin, Bering, Bhawani Gautam, Billylikeswikis, BirdbrainedPhoenix, Bobblewik, Cacophony, Capricorn42, Captain-n00dle, Carnildo, Carre, Charliearcuri, ChrisUK, Conti, Conversion script, Crashmatrix, CryptoDerk, Cvgs 0007, DaedalusRaistlin, Dafocus, Davidisom, Dawnseeker2000, Dcarriso, Defeatedfear, Dennis Bratland, Depictionimage, DerHexer, Dgtsyb, Diannaa, DoubleBlue, Dr. Zaret, Dysprosia, EagleOne, EdoDodo, Edward, Email4mobile, EnTheMohammad, Engineerism, Ergosteur, Esnible, Europrobe, Euryalus, Evergreen9, EwaDuan, Extraordinary, FH 3, Fleminra, Frazzydee, Fuzheado, Gaius Cornelius, Gjivan, Gzkn, Hadal, Hadiyana, Hallje, HamburgerRadio, Hede2000, Hemanshu, Hgonzale, Hhan, Hohum, Hydrargyrum, IGeMiNix, INkubusse, Iandiver, Inter, Intgr, Inzy, Jackerhack, Jacooks, Jasonauk, Jemuel, Jim.henderson, Jklin, Jnavas, Jonathanriddell, Joseph Solis in Australia, KB1KOI, Karada, Karl.brown, KingOfSofa, Kmbsww, Ksn, Learns visits aw, Lerdsuwa, Leszek Jańczuk, LeviathinXII, Liftarn, Lightmouse, LoopZilla, Luen, MC MasterChef, MER-C, Mac, Mange01, Manumg, Mathiastck, Maximus Rex, Mentifisto, Michael Hardy, Mike Rosoft, Mittosi, Mojodaddy, Monty Dickerson, Mozzerati, NOYKG, NPalmius, Nageh, Nakon, Neale Monks, Nil Einne, Nmnogueira, Novldp, Nwynder, Ohnoitsjamie, Oli Filth, Omegatron, One half 3544, Palopt, Pan Camel, Patrick, Pb30, Pbook8989, PeteVerdon, Pgan002, PhilHibbs, Piano non troppo, Plamka, Plasmaroo, Pmuschi, Pratyeka, Prolog, Qasdfdsaq, RHaworth, Radiojon, Rajeshnawal, Raohammad, Requestion, Rettetast, Rich257, Richardcraib, Ricky lais, Rjstott, Roberts83, Seancdaug, Seaphoto, Seikku Kaita, Sesu Prime, Shadowjams, Shahzad11, Shinpah1, Silvermane, Slashme, Smalljim, Smhanov, Smsarmad, SpaceFlight89, Spel-Punc-Gram, Starszz, Stevehughes, Stinkinrich88, Stuart Ward UK, Sudeeprg, Svinodh, Swhitehead, Tex23, The Thing That Should Not Be, Thierry Bingen, Thue, Tom Morris, Tombomp, Tommike125, Tommy2010, Tooki, Trevor MacInnis, TutterMouse, Tyz, Utuado, Vegaswikian, Vipul, Vk2tds, Wapxana, Wik, WikiSysop2, Wikiliki, Winged-stone, Wo.luren, Woohookitty, Wrs1864, Wtmitchell, Youssefsan, Yury Tarasievich, Zzedar, Саша Стефановић, Ὁ οἶστρος, 497 anonymous edits

Image Sources, Licenses and Contributors

File:Wireshark screenshot.png *Source*: http://en.wikipedia.org/w/index.php?title=File:Wireshark_screenshot.png *License*: unknown *Contributors*: uploader

File:FLETC Glynco-aerial.gif *Source*: http://en.wikipedia.org/w/index.php?title=File:FLETC_Glynco-aerial.gif *License*: unknown *Contributors*: Drug Enforcement Administration (DEA), a United States Department of Justice law enforcement agency

Image:Portable forensic tableau.JPG *Source*: http://en.wikipedia.org/w/index.php?title=File:Portable_forensic_tableau.JPG *License*: unknown *Contributors*: User:ErrantX

Image:En exif data.png *Source*: http://en.wikipedia.org/w/index.php?title=File:En_exif_data.png *License*: unknown *Contributors*: User:SreeBot

Image:PersonalStorageDevices.agr.jpg *Source*: http://en.wikipedia.org/w/index.php?title=File:PersonalStorageDevices.agr.jpg *License*: unknown *Contributors*: User:ArnoldReinhold

Image:Mobiles.JPG *Source*: http://en.wikipedia.org/w/index.php?title=File:Mobiles.JPG *License*: unknown *Contributors*: Errant

File:Internet map 1024.jpg *Source*: http://en.wikipedia.org/w/index.php?title=File:Internet_map_1024.jpg *License*: unknown *Contributors*: Barrett Lyon The Opte Project

File:Distributed Processing.jpg *Source*: http://en.wikipedia.org/w/index.php?title=File:Distributed_Processing.jpg *License*: unknown *Contributors*: User:Bp2010.hprastiawan

Image:NETWORK-Library-LAN.png *Source*: http://en.wikipedia.org/w/index.php?title=File:NETWORK-Library-LAN.png *License*: unknown *Contributors*: User:Hcberkowitz

File:EPN Frame-Relay and Dial-up Network.svg *Source*: http://en.wikipedia.org/w/index.php?title=File:EPN_Frame-Relay_and_Dial-up_Network.svg *License*: unknown *Contributors*: Ludovic.ferre

File:Virtual Private Network overview.svg *Source*: http://en.wikipedia.org/w/index.php?title=File:Virtual_Private_Network_overview.svg *License*: unknown *Contributors*: Ludovic.ferre

File:Network Overlay.svg *Source*: http://en.wikipedia.org/w/index.php?title=File:Network_Overlay.svg *License*: unknown *Contributors*: Ludovic.ferre]]

Image:PD-icon.svg *Source*: http://en.wikipedia.org/w/index.php?title=File:PD-icon.svg *License*: unknown *Contributors*: Alex.muller, Anomie, Anonymous Dissident, CBM, MBisanz, Quadell, Rocket000, Strangerer, Timotheus Canens, 1 anonymous edits

File:PersonalStorageDevices.agr.jpg *Source*: http://en.wikipedia.org/w/index.php?title=File:PersonalStorageDevices.agr.jpg *License*: unknown *Contributors*: User:ArnoldReinhold

File:Portable forensic tableau.JPG *Source*: http://en.wikipedia.org/w/index.php?title=File:Portable_forensic_tableau.JPG *License*: unknown *Contributors*: User:ErrantX

Image:Ethernet RJ45 connector p1160054.jpg *Source*: http://en.wikipedia.org/w/index.php?title=File:Ethernet_RJ45_connector_p1160054.jpg *License*: unknown *Contributors*: User:David.Monniaux

File:Loudspeaker.svg *Source*: http://en.wikipedia.org/w/index.php?title=File:Loudspeaker.svg *License*: unknown *Contributors*: Bayo, Gmaxwell, Husky, Iamunknown, Mirithing, Myself488, Nethac DIU, Omegatron, Rocket000, The Evil IP address, Wouterhagens, 18 anonymous edits

File:10Base5transcievers.jpg *Source*: http://en.wikipedia.org/w/index.php?title=File:10Base5transcievers.jpg *License*: unknown *Contributors*: Original uploader was Robert.Harker at en.wikipedia

Image:Network card.jpg *Source*: http://en.wikipedia.org/w/index.php?title=File:Network_card.jpg *License*: unknown *Contributors*: User:Nixdorf

File:Network switches.jpg *Source*: http://en.wikipedia.org/w/index.php?title=File:Network_switches.jpg *License*: unknown *Contributors*: User:ShakataGaNai

File:Coreswitch (2634205113).jpg *Source*: http://en.wikipedia.org/w/index.php?title=File:Coreswitch_(2634205113).jpg *License*: unknown *Contributors*: Dave Fischer

File:UDP encapsulation.svg *Source*: http://en.wikipedia.org/w/index.php?title=File:UDP_encapsulation.svg *License*: unknown *Contributors*: original work, colorization by

Image:Huawei E220 (Three).jpg *Source*: http://en.wikipedia.org/w/index.php?title=File:Huawei_E220_(Three).jpg *License*: unknown *Contributors*: User:Korax1214

GNU Free Documentation License Version 1.2, November 2002 Copyright (C) 2000,2001,2002 Free Software Foundation, Inc. 59 Temple Place, Suite 330, Boston, MA 02111-1307 USA Everyone is permitted to copy and distribute verbatim copies of this license document, but changing it is not allowed.

0. PREAMBLE

The purpose of this License is to make a manual, textbook, or other functional and useful document "free" in the sense of freedom: to assure everyone the effective freedom to copy and redistribute it, with or without modifying it, either commercially or noncommercially. Secondarily, this License preserves for the author and publisher a way to get credit for their work, while not being considered responsible for modifications made by others. This License is a kind of "copyleft", which means that derivative works of the document must themselves be free in the same sense. It complements the GNU General Public License, which is a copyleft license designed for free software. We have designed this License in order to use it for manuals for free software, because free software needs free documentation: a free program should come with manuals providing the same freedoms that the software does. But this License is not limited to software manuals; it can be used for any textual work, regardless of subject matter or whether it is published as a printed book. We recommend this License principally for works whose purpose is instruction or reference.

1. APPLICABILITY AND DEFINITIONS

This License applies to any manual or other work, in any medium, that contains a notice placed by the copyright holder saying it can be distributed under the terms of this License. Such a notice grants a world-wide, royalty-free license, unlimited in duration, to use that work under the conditions stated herein. The "Document", below, refers to any such manual or work. Any member of the public is a licensee, and is addressed as "you". You accept the license if you copy, modify or distribute the work in a way requiring permission under copyright law. A "Modified Version" of the Document means any work containing the Document or a portion of it, either copied verbatim, or with modifications and/or translated into another language. A "Secondary Section" is a named appendix or a front-matter section of the Document that deals exclusively with the relationship of the publishers or authors of the Document to the Document's overall subject (or to related matters) and contains nothing that could fall directly within that overall subject. (Thus, if the Document is in part a textbook of mathematics, a Secondary Section may not explain any mathematics.) The relationship could be a matter of historical connection with the subject or with related matters, or of legal, commercial, philosophical, ethical or political position regarding them. The "Invariant Sections" are certain Secondary Sections whose titles are designated, as being those of Invariant Sections, in the notice that says that the Document is released under this License. If a section does not fit the above definition of Secondary then it is not allowed to be designated as Invariant. The Document may contain zero Invariant Sections. If the Document does not identify any Invariant Sections then there are none. The "Cover Texts" are certain short passages of text that are listed, as Front-Cover Texts or Back-Cover Texts, in the notice that says that the Document is released under this License. A Front-Cover Text may be at most 5 words, and a Back-Cover Text may be at most 25 words. A "Transparent" copy of the Document means a machine-readable copy, represented in a format whose specification is available to the general public, that is suitable for revising the document straightforwardly with generic text editors or (for images composed of pixels) generic paint programs or (for drawings) some widely available drawing editor, and that is suitable for input to text formatters or for automatic translation to a variety of formats suitable for input to text formatters. A copy made in an otherwise Transparent file format whose markup, or absence of markup, has been arranged to thwart or discourage subsequent modification by readers is not Transparent. An image format is not Transparent if used for any substantial amount of text. A copy that is not "Transparent" is called "Opaque". Examples of suitable formats for Transparent copies include plain ASCII without markup, Texinfo input format, LaTeX input format, SGML or XML using a publicly available DTD, and standard-conforming simple HTML, PostScript or PDF designed for human modification. Examples of transparent image formats include PNG, XCF and JPG. Opaque formats include proprietary formats that can be read and edited only by proprietary word processors, SGML or XML for which the DTD and/or processing tools are not generally available, and the machine-generated HTML, PostScript or PDF produced by some word processors for output purposes only. The "Title Page" means, for a printed book, the title page itself, plus such following pages as are needed to hold, legibly, the material this License requires to appear in the title page. For works in formats which do not have any title page as such, "Title Page" means the text near the most prominent appearance of the work's title, preceding the beginning of the body of the text. A section "Entitled XYZ" means a named subunit of the Document whose title either is precisely XYZ or contains XYZ in parentheses following text that translates XYZ in another language. (Here XYZ stands for a specific section name mentioned below, such as "Acknowledgements", "Dedications", "Endorsements", or "History".) To "Preserve the Title" of such a section when you modify the Document means that it remains a section "Entitled XYZ" according to this definition. The Document may include Warranty Disclaimers next to the notice which states that this License applies to the Document. These Warranty Disclaimers are considered to be included by reference in this License, but only as regards disclaiming warranties: any other implication that these Warranty Disclaimers may have is void and has no effect on the meaning of this License.

2. VERBATIM COPYING

You may copy and distribute the Document in any medium, either commercially or noncommercially, provided that this License, the copyright notices, and the license notice saying this License applies to the Document are reproduced in all copies, and that you add no other conditions whatsoever to those of this License. You may not use technical measures to obstruct or control the reading or further copying of the copies you make or distribute. However, you may accept compensation in exchange for copies. If you distribute a large enough number of copies you must also follow the conditions in section 3. You may also lend copies, under the same conditions stated above, and you may publicly display copies.

3. COPYING IN QUANTITY

If you publish printed copies (or copies in media that commonly have printed covers) of the Document, numbering more than 100, and the Document's license notice requires Cover Texts, you must enclose the copies in covers that carry, clearly and legibly, all these Cover Texts: Front-Cover Texts on the front cover, and Back-Cover Texts on the back cover. Both covers must also clearly and legibly identify you as the publisher of these copies. The front cover must present the full title with all words of the title equally prominent and visible. You may add other material on the covers in addition. Copying with changes limited to the covers, as long as they preserve the title of the Document and satisfy these conditions, can be treated as verbatim copying in other respects. If the required texts for either cover are too voluminous to fit legibly, you should put the first ones listed (as many as fit reasonably) on the actual cover, and continue the rest onto adjacent pages. If you publish or distribute Opaque copies of the Document numbering more than 100, you must either include a machine-readable Transparent copy along with each Opaque copy, or state in or with each Opaque copy a computer-network location from which the general network-using public has access to download using public-standard network protocols a complete Transparent copy of the Document, free of added material. If you use the latter option, you must take reasonably prudent steps, when you begin distribution of Opaque copies in quantity, to ensure that this Transparent copy will remain thus accessible at the stated location until at least one year after the last time you distribute an Opaque copy (directly or through your agents or retailers) of that edition to the public. It is requested, but not required, that you contact the authors of the Document well before redistributing any large number of copies, to give them a chance to provide you with an updated version of the Document.

4. MODIFICATIONS

You may copy and distribute a Modified Version of the Document under the conditions of sections 2 and 3 above, provided that you release the Modified Version under precisely this License, with the Modified Version filling the role of the Document, thus licensing distribution and modification of the Modified Version to whoever possesses a copy of it. In addition, you must do these things in the Modified Version: A. Use in the Title Page (and on the covers, if any) a title distinct from that of the Document, and from those of previous versions (which should, if there were any, be listed in the History section of the Document). You may use the same title as a previous version if the original publisher of that version gives permission. B. List on the Title Page, as authors, one or more persons or entities responsible for authorship of the modifications in the Modified Version, together with at least five of the principal authors of the Document (all of its principal authors, if it has fewer than five), unless they release you from this requirement. C. State on the Title page the name of the publisher of the Modified Version, as the publisher. D. Preserve all the copyright notices of the Document. E. Add an appropriate copyright notice for your modifications adjacent to the other copyright notices. F. Include, immediately after the copyright notices, a license notice giving the public permission to use the Modified Version under the terms of this License, in the form shown in the Addendum below. G. Preserve in that license notice the full lists of Invariant Sections and required Cover Texts given in the Document's license notice. H. Include an unaltered copy of this License. I. Preserve the section Entitled "History", Preserve its Title, and add to it an item stating at least the title, year, new authors, and publisher of the Modified Version as given on the Title Page. If there is no section Entitled "History" in the Document, create one stating the title, year, authors, and publisher of the Document as given on its Title Page, then add an item describing the Modified Version as stated in the previous sentence. J. Preserve the network location, if any, given in the Document for public access to a Transparent copy of the Document, and likewise the network locations given in the Document for previous versions it was based on. These may be placed in the "History" section. You may omit a network location for a work that was published at least four years before the Document itself, or if the original publisher of the version it refers to gives permission. K. For any section Entitled "Acknowledgements" or "Dedications", Preserve the Title of the section, and preserve in the section all the substance and tone of each of the contributor acknowledgements and/or dedications given therein. L. Preserve all the Invariant Sections of the Document, unaltered in their text and in their titles. Section numbers or the equivalent are not considered part of the section titles. M. Delete any section Entitled "Endorsements". Such a section may not be included in the Modified Version. N. Do not retitle any existing section to be Entitled "Endorsements" or to conflict in title with any Invariant Section. O. Preserve any Warranty Disclaimers. If the Modified Version includes new front-matter sections or appendices that qualify as Secondary Sections and contain no material copied from the Document, you may at your option designate some or all of these sections as invariant. To do this, add their titles to the list of Invariant Sections in the Modified Version's license notice. These titles must be distinct from any other section titles. You may add a section Entitled "Endorsements", provided it contains nothing but endorsements of your Modified Version by various parties--for example, statements of peer review or that the text has been approved by an organization as the authoritative definition of a standard. You may add a passage of up to five words as a Front-Cover Text, and a passage of up to 25 words as a Back-Cover Text, to the end of the list of Cover Texts in the Modified Version. Only one passage of Front-Cover Text and one of Back-Cover Text may be added by (or through arrangements made by) any one entity. If the Document already includes a cover text for the same cover, previously added by you or by arrangement made by the same entity you are acting on behalf of, you may not add another; but you may replace the old one, on explicit permission from the previous publisher that added the old one. The author(s) and publisher(s) of the Document do not by this License give permission to use their names for publicity for or to assert or imply endorsement of any Modified Version.

5. COMBINING DOCUMENTS

You may combine the Document with other documents released under this License, under the terms defined in section 4 above for modified versions, provided that you include in the combination all of the Invariant Sections of all of the original documents, unmodified, and list them all as Invariant Sections of your combined work in its license notice, and that you preserve all their Warranty Disclaimers. The combined work need only contain one copy of this License, and multiple identical Invariant Sections may be replaced with a single copy. If there are multiple Invariant Sections with the same name but different contents, make the title of each such section unique by adding at the end of it, in parentheses, the name of the original author or publisher of that section if known, or else a unique number. Make the same adjustment to the section titles in the list of Invariant Sections in the license notice of the combined work. In the combination, you must combine any sections Entitled "History" in the various original documents, forming one section Entitled "History"; likewise combine any sections Entitled "Acknowledgements", and any sections Entitled "Dedications". You must delete all sections Entitled "Endorsements".

6. COLLECTIONS OF DOCUMENTS

You may make a collection consisting of the Document and other documents released under this License, and replace the individual copies of this License in the various documents with a single copy that is included in the collection, provided that you follow the rules of this License for verbatim copying of each of the documents in all other respects. You may extract a single document from such a collection, and distribute it individually under this License, provided you insert a copy of this License into the extracted document, and follow this License in all other respects regarding verbatim copying of that document.

7. AGGREGATION WITH INDEPENDENT WORKS

A compilation of the Document or its derivatives with other separate and independent documents or works, in or on a volume of a storage or distribution medium, is called an "aggregate" if the copyright resulting from the compilation is not used to limit the legal rights of the compilation's users beyond what the individual works permit. When the Document is included in an aggregate, this License does not apply to the other works in the aggregate which are not themselves derivative works of the Document. If the Cover Text requirement of section 3 is applicable to these copies of the Document, then if the Document is less than one half of the entire aggregate, the Document's Cover Texts may be placed on covers that bracket the Document within the aggregate, or the electronic equivalent of covers if the Document is in electronic form. Otherwise they must appear on printed covers that bracket the whole aggregate.

8. TRANSLATION

Translation is considered a kind of modification, so you may distribute translations of the Document under the terms of section 4. Replacing Invariant Sections with translations requires special permission from their copyright holders, but you may include translations of some or all Invariant Sections in addition to the original versions of these Invariant Sections. You may include a translation of this License, and all the license notices in the Document, and any Warranty Disclaimers, provided that you also include the original English version of this License and the original versions of those notices and disclaimers. In case of a disagreement between the translation and the original version of this License or a notice or disclaimer, the original version will prevail. If a section in the Document is Entitled "Acknowledgements", "Dedications", or "History", the requirement (section 4) to Preserve its Title (section 1) will typically require changing the actual title.

9. TERMINATION

You may not copy, modify, sublicense, or distribute the Document except as expressly provided for under this License. Any other attempt to copy, modify, sublicense or distribute the Document is void, and will automatically terminate your rights under this License. However, parties who have received copies, or rights, from you under this License will not have their licenses terminated so long as such parties remain in full compliance.

10. FUTURE REVISIONS OF THIS LICENSE

The Free Software Foundation may publish new, revised versions of the GNU Free Documentation License from time to time. Such new versions will be similar in spirit to the present version, but may differ in detail to address new problems or concerns. See http://www.gnu.org/copyleft/. Each version of the License is given a distinguishing version number. If the Document specifies that a particular numbered version of this License "or any later version" applies to it, you have the option of following the terms and conditions either of that specified version or of any later version that has been published (not as a draft) by the Free Software Foundation. If the Document does not specify a version number of this License, you may choose any version ever published (not as a draft) by the Free Software Foundation. ADDENDUM: How to use this License for your documents To use this License in a document you have written, include a copy of the License in the document and put the following copyright and license notices just after the title page: Copyright (c) YEAR YOUR NAME. Permission is granted to copy, distribute and/or modify this document under the terms of the GNU Free Documentation License, Version 1.2 or any later version published by the Free Software Foundation; with no Invariant Sections, no Front-Cover Texts, and no Back-Cover Texts. A copy of the license is included in the section entitled "GNU Free Documentation License". If you have Invariant Sections, Front-Cover Texts and Back-Cover Texts, replace the "with...Texts." line with this: with the Invariant Sections being LIST THEIR TITLES, with the Front-Cover Texts being LIST, and with the Back-Cover Texts being LIST. If you have Invariant Sections without Cover Texts, or some other combination of the three, merge those two alternatives to suit the situation. If your document contains nontrivial examples of program code, we recommend releasing these examples in parallel under your choice of free software license, such as the GNU General Public License, to permit their use in free software.

Printed by Books on Demand GmbH, Norderstedt / Germany